D1538566

Firesetting Children:
Risk Assessment and Treatment

GEORGE A. SAKHEIM
ELIZABETH OSBORN

Child Welfare League of America
Washington, DC

© 1994 by the Child Welfare League of America, Inc.

All rights reserved. Neither this book nor any part may be reproduced or transmitted in any form or by any means, electronic or mechanical, including photocopying, microfilming, and recording, or by any information storage and retrieval system, without permission in writing from the publisher. For information on this or other CWLA publications, contact the CWLA Publications Department at the address below.

Child Welfare League of America, Inc.
440 First Street, NW, Suite 310, Washington, DC 20001-2085

Current Printing (last digit)
10 9 8 7 6 5 4 3 2 1

Cover design by Paul H. Butler
Text design by Deborah Finette

Printed in the United States of America

ISBN # 0-87868-579-0

Contents

Foreword

It is well known that children, especially boys, are curious about fire and that a significant number engage in exploratory fire play. For some, unfortunately, such activity evolves into chronic firesetting, with a resultant enormous destruction of property and, not infrequently, loss of life. Yet the problem of explicitly assessing and identifying those juveniles at great risk for recidivism in firesetting has been conspicuously under-studied. This significant void has been essentially remedied by the present authors, who have produced a book providing specific guidelines for differentiating chronic, severe firesetting from less serious forms.

Drawing on careful investigation spanning 12 years and five studies of firesetters, they have admirably combined an insightful psychodynamic approach with stringent principles of research design entailing closely matched controls and comprehensive data analyses. A unique feature of the book is a worksheet developed for conducting a firesetting appraisal and then arriving at a prediction equation, which in the last of their five studies proved to be 96% accurate. Utilizing information gleaned from an intelligence scale, a projective battery, interview and case history data, and even school reports and nursing notes, the clinician can rate various indicators on this worksheet as *present, absent,* or *don't know.* If the majority of the indicators are present, a substantial risk is present in terms of a configurational firesetter profile. Items tapping behavioral controls and ego strengths are also included. The authors provide many excellent examples to assist in the scoring of worksheet indicators.

Among other especially useful features of this book are the extensive and critical review of the literature on firesetting, a section on how to interview a child to get at motivations in starting fires, and a highly articulate discussion of treatment and placement issues. Attesting to the expertise and broad experience of the authors is the richness of their interpretations of the clinical material, skillfully and systematically integrated with the research findings throughout this volume.

This well-balanced, clearly written work would be an important source of information for any professional involved in the process of firesetting risk determination. Apart from its focus on firesetting per se, most impressive to this writer are the probing, dynamic evaluations of Rorschach content. Thus, this book could be read with considerable profit by any clinician interested in learning how to utilize content analysis of projective responses in the most productive manner.

Marvin Reznikoff, Ph.D.

Professor of Psychology
Fordham University

Preface

This volume is intended for use by psychologists, clinical social workers, and psychiatrists to aid them in distinguishing between juvenile firesetters and nonfiresetters, and between low-risk match players or curiosity firesetters and high-risk or pathological firesetters. It describes those personality and behavioral characteristics and family background factors that have been consistently and positively associated with firesetting behavior. It demonstrates how a firesetter risk evaluation may be performed.

A careful reading of the child's case record, followed by specific testing and a sensitive interview, will provide the clinician with the data necessary to code the worksheet for the presence or absence of the relevant variables. In order to code the 14 items constituting the prediction equation, the clinician should elicit all the data that are not specifically provided in the clinical reports (such as the social history, psychological evaluation, psychiatric examination, child care report, school report, and nursing notes) from the child and from parents, therapists, or child care staff members who know the child well.

Once the data have been coded on the worksheet, it becomes easy to calculate the prediction equation. The results inform the clinician whether a particular child's profile more closely resembles that of the severe high-risk or the nonsevere low-risk firesetter group. The results also highlight the dynamics of and the motivations for each particular firesetting incident. They address both the fire set in the community and the fire within the child. The section on scoring aids, in chapter 2, illustrates in specific, concrete terms how to score the variables in the prediction equation that make up the psychological profile of the juvenile firesetter. Chapter 3 summarizes valuable approaches and proven techniques for treating four categories of firesetters in the community and/or in the residential treatment center. To illustrate the application of these techniques, chapter 4 presents a case example of the analysis of a severe firesetter with specific recommendations for placement and treatment. Finally, the appendix gives brief case examples of what the authors consider to be severe and nonsevere firesetters.

Acknowledgments

Dr. Osborn and I are greatly indebted to the Jewish Child Care Association of New York for its enduring support of this body of research. Particularly, we would like to thank David Roth, Dr. Paul Gitelson, Richard Altman, John Stadler, M.D., and Dr. Franklin Goldberg for their assistance in carrying out the necessary studies at the Association's Pleasantville Cottage School and the Pleasantville Diagnostic Center. The help of the late Bernice Falk is warmly remembered. Dr. Beverly Richard and Dr. David Sakheim, our statistical consultants, were of invaluable help in the completion of the data analysis.

We would like to take this opportunity to acknowledge our debt to the many colleagues who contributed their ideas to the creation of this volume in staff meetings at Pleasantville and in workshops and conferences in the Westchester community.

During the process of revising and rewriting this manuscript we sent copies to 10 respected colleagues who are senior members of their professions. Six are practicing clinical psychologists, three are clinical social workers who supervise and teach graduate students at hospitals or universities, and one is a child psychiatrist. They served as peer reviewers for this volume. We wish to express our special gratitude to these colleagues for having taken the time out of their busy schedules to provide the benefit of their experience, their suggestions, and their constructive criticisms. Many of their reactions and suggestions were incorporated into the final version of the manuscript. They are: Paul Fuller, Ph.D.; Leo Katz, Ph.D.; Raymond Parker, Ph.D.; Nancy Peters, M.D.; Marvin Reznikoff, Ph.D.; Ilse Sakheim, A.C.S.W.; Lorraine Siegel, D.S.W.; Arthur Swanson, Ph.D.; Martin Vigdor, Ph.D.; and Nancy Webb, D.S.W.

We also wish to acknowledge the excellent organizing and typing skills of Ms. Tina Bailey, during the different stages of the development of the manuscript.

As the undersigned, my deepest gratitude goes to my wife, Ilse, for sharing my concerns and my hopes during the year that we worked on putting together this volume. Since her partial retirement from the practice of social work, we have formed yet another partnership, and now do firesetter risk evaluations together as a team.

Finally, Dr. Osborn and I wish to express our appreciation to Carl Schoenberg, our editor at the Child Welfare League, whose encouragement, high standards, and thoroughness transformed a manuscript into a book.

George A. Sakheim

The Five Research Studies: Chronology and Summary of Findings

CHRONOLOGY OF FIRESETTER RESEARCH FOR THIS VOLUME

- Study I—1982-1984. "A Psychological Profile of Juvenile Firesetters in Residential Treatment." George A. Sakheim; Martin G. Vigdor; Melissa Gordon; & Leslie M. Helprin. Sample: 30 firesetters and 15 nonfiresetters. *CHILD WELFARE* LXIV, 5 (September-October 1985): 453–476.

- Study II—1984-1985. "A Psychological Profile of Juvenile Firesetters in Residential Treatment: A Replication Study." George A. Sakheim and Elizabeth Osborn. Sample: 20 firesetters and 20 nonfiresetters. *CHILD WELFARE* LXV, 5 (September-October 1986): 495–503.

- Study III—1989-1990. "Toward a Clearer Differentiation of High-Risk from Low-Risk Firesetters." George A. Sakheim; Elizabeth Osborn; & David Abrams. Sample: 25 Severe firesetters and 25 minor firesetters. *CHILD WELFARE* LXX, 4 (July-August 1991): 489–503.

- Study IV—1990-1991. Comparing 50 Severe or High-Risk with 50 Minor or Low-Risk Firesetters. George A. Sakheim and Elizabeth Osborn. Reported in this volume.

- Study V—1992. Comparing 50 Severe Firesetters with 105 Minor and Nonfiresetters. George A. Sakheim and Elizabeth Osborn. Reported in this volume.

This volume brings to a close a 12-year quest for valid and reliable criteria that would identify the child who may be seriously at risk for setting fires in his or her home, at school, or in the community. From our series of research studies, we have been able to identify such a set of indicators or criteria [Sakheim et al. 1985; Sakheim and Osborn 1986; Sakheim et al. 1991].

The methodology described in this volume was developed to help psychologists and other mental health professionals improve the accuracy of their evaluation of the critical factors for recidivism when assessing juvenile fire-setters. Specifically, the authors' research program has culminated in a statistically derived prediction equation for the classification of firesetters into *severe* and *nonsevere* subgroups. Also, correlational analyses describe frequency differences on 36 salient variables across *nonfiresetter, minor fire-setter,* and *severe firesetter* groups totaling 155 subjects.

National statistics indicate that juveniles under the age of 18 are responsible for approximately 60% of all fires set in large cities [Juvenile Firesetter Intervention Program 1989]. Many of these child firesetters are under nine years of age, and a remarkable number are four-year-old boys, according to two studies in two different New York State locations [Cole et al. 1986; JFIP 1988]. In the literature, boys far outnumber girls; the ratio of male to female firesetters has been found rather consistently to be in the neighbor-hood of nine to one [Kolko 1985: 356].*

Wooden and Berkey reported [1984, cited in Kolko 1989]: "Arson is the fastest growing crime in the U.S., and it is also the most costly. Of the nearly 3 million fires reported across the country, almost 1 in 5 is committed by a juvenile." Recent uniform crime reports indicate that juveniles account for 40% of arson arrests and convictions [U.S. Federal Bureau of Investigation 1987]. Many more firesetters are never caught or arrested, and therefore do not come to the attention of legal authorities.

We first became interested in the study of juvenile firesetters in 1980, after three residents had set three separate destructive fires at the resi-dential treatment center where the senior author was chief psychologist. Initially, we were interested primarily in identifying at the point of intake those children with firesetting in their histories whose pattern was deeply ingrained (recurrent, intentional, with no guilt or remorse present), and who therefore presented a danger to the other children and the staff. After our negative experiences, it was decided to keep such children out of the treatment center.

By 1983, as we gained experience with the psychological profile of the juve-nile firesetter and no more fires had been set, we began to admit those children who we felt needed our services and whom we could serve therapeutically without endangering others. These were primarily accidental or curiosity fire-setters—children who had set a fire or two in an attempt to attract attention to

---

* Note: Because of this gender predominance and for ease in reading, the pronoun *he* is used throughout this volume when gender is not otherwise specified.

themselves or to utter a cry for help. By 1988, 35 such children had been admitted to the treatment center and not one of them had set a fire.

We attributed this successful record to advances in both our ability to screen out dangerous firesetters and our experience in the treatment and management of the less severe firesetters. The removal of the child from a noxious or abusive home environment and the center's structure, supervision, therapeutic support, and nurturance helped eliminate firesetting behavior in the less severe group.

Three factors—removal from home; careful screening at intake to rule out the aggressive, delinquent, antisocial firesetter who is lacking in empathy, uses fire as a weapon against adult authority, and shows no guilt or remorse about previous acts of firesetting; and increased understanding of appropriate interventions in the treatment of the children who were accepted—led to the positive results. Because other agencies have expressed interest in the center's approach and methods and requested consultation, this volume reports what has been learned from our program of systematic research with these difficult children.

CATEGORIES AND DEFINITIONS

Grolnick and her associates wrote in 1990:

> The few studies examining normative samples have suggested the almost universal nature of fire interest in children [Block & Block 1975]. One study addressed the prevalence of fire-play in a normative sample. Kafrey [1980] interviewed 99 five-to-nine year old boys about their fire-play. More than 40% had engaged in fire-play. Only 9% of the incidents the boys were involved with were reported to the fire department. Although not disturbed, the children who played with fire were reported by their parents to be more disobedient and have more accidents than those who did not play.

In a survey of 770 school children ages six to 14 years [Grolnick et al. 1990], "38% of the children indicated that they had at some point played with fire, and 14% indicated that they had played with fire since the beginning of the current school year." Thus, fire-play motivated by curiosity is really quite common among young children, especially among boys.

In their comprehensive study of 104 firesetters who were apprehended and processed by authorities in San Bernadino County, California, Wooden and Berkey [1984: 23-24] used four broad, practical categories to classify firesetters:

1. Curious or playing-with-matches firesetters,
2. Troubled or "crying for help" firesetters,
3. Delinquent firesetters, and
4. Pathological or seriously disturbed firesetters.

In a general way, we have followed this practical classification system. For the sake of greater precision or refinement, however, subcategories have been added that were derived from other important studies cited in the literature.

In 1992 we conducted a statistical analysis of two groups, totaling 155 children, that compared 50 minor firesetters and 55 nonfiresetters with 50 severe firesetters. A prediction equation derived from this analysis classified group membership with 96% accuracy. Additionally, the three groups—nonfiresetters, minor firesetters, and major firesetters—were compared on 36 variables via a correlational analysis.

For purposes of this analysis, a minor firesetter was defined as a child, usually under the age of 10, whose firesetting was prompted by curiosity, by playing with matches or lighters, by exploring his environment, or by mischievous attention seeking. The important distinction is that the resulting fire occurred accidentally and that the child did not intend to be destructive or to do any damage to life or property. The severe or major firesetter group consisted of children and adolescents between the ages of five and 17 who engaged in intentional, purposeful, and recurrent firesetting (pathological firesetting). The mean number of fires set by members of the minor group was two, while the mean number for the severe group was four. Thus, children in the severe group had a history of setting more fires as well as more serious fires.

The nonfiresetter control group consisted of 55 children drawn from the same population of residents in a residential treatment center and children evaluated in a diagnostic center for Persons In Need of Supervision (PINS) on the grounds of the residential treatment center. A careful reading of their case records, which included a recent (within the year) psychological assessment, a current psychiatric evaluation, a social history, and school reports, showed no evidence that any of the children in the control group had ever set a fire, either accidentally or deliberately. Two researchers read the case records independently, and if there was any evidence of fire-play or firesetting, the child was disqualified from serving as a control subject. In other words, the case records of the 55 control subjects were "clean" as regards any evidence of firesetting tendencies. Having such a control group is vital in research of this kind because it helps to discriminate antisocial or delinquent firesetting from other types of delinquent behavior.

SUMMARY: RESULTS OF THE FIVE RESEARCH STUDIES

Study I

The first step in our earliest investigation was a thorough search of the clinical and research literature for hypotheses about firesetting. This search yielded 80 variables that were alleged to describe juvenile firesetters at that time. The next step was a systematic assessment of which of these variables held up in controlled investigation to determine whether juveniles in residential treatment would show such factors [Sakheim et al. 1985]. Each factor was operationally defined so that profiles of the children could be examined for its presence or absence. Controlled comparisons were the next step, in order to isolate the factors that truly related to firesetting, rather than to all children in residential treatment or to acting-out delinquents in general. Lastly, we became increasingly interested in those factors that could discriminate the severe or pathological firesetter from the minor or less severe case, since this is usually the most salient question at intake. The database increased over a 12-year period from the original 30 to the present 200 cases.

Thus, the research perspective began with a global input from many sources, theories, and models in the search for variables that other investigators considered important. The focus was progressively narrowed to determine first, which variables held up as part of a firesetter profile, and then which variables could discriminate firesetters from other delinquents or children with other acting-out conduct disorders. Finally, we arrived at the variables that could discriminate severe firesetters from less dangerous children, those appropriate for most residential treatment centers.

From our search of the literature, it appeared that no single concept could adequately explain why children set fires. Our observations confirmed this research. Firesetting is a complex and overdetermined act. A number of overlapping motivations are often active at the same time.

To discern the most salient and possibly predictive variables associated with firesetting, Sakheim et al. [1985] examined the records of 30 emotionally disturbed firesetters in residential treatment in light of the 80 variables derived from the clinical literature. When these known firesetters were compared with a matched group of nonfiresetters, 14 statistically significant variables emerged. The following nine characteristics were present most often among the firesetters, and discriminate reliably between the two groups: (1) the presence of pleasurable or sexual excitement when lighting or watching a fire; (2) intense anger at the mother for rejecting, emotionally depriving, or abandoning the child; (3) anger at the father for being unavailable, abusive, or abandoning the family, or for having died; (4) the tendency to respond to a narcissistic injury with rage and fantasies of revenge; (5) gaining power over adults by setting fires; (6) sexual conflicts or sexual dysfunction; (7) poor judgment in social situations; (8) difficulty in verbalizing anger; and (9) psychiatric diagnosis of conduct disorder.

Study II

Sakheim and Osborn [1986] used a similar methodology in examining the clinical records of 20 additional firesetters and 20 nonfiresetters in a residential treatment center. In this study, the authors found that the following variables differentiated between the two groups: (1) anger at the mother for severe maternal rejection; (2) anger at the father for abandonment or for abuse; (3) fantasies of revenge; (4) rage at insults; (5) sadistic or destructive themes; (6) sexual excitement; (7) projection of fire or explosion responses on projective tests; (8) impulsivity; (9) inadequate superego development; and (10) a psychiatric diagnosis of conduct disorder [APA 1980, DSM-III]. These results are essentially consistent with and augment the earlier findings of Sakheim et al. 1985.

Study III

Study III, completed in 1990, was a response to the challenge presented in consulting practice to differentiate between subgroups of firesetters. It proposed to identify different levels of risk for recidivism that have been associated with the various subgroups. The principal subgroups described in the literature include the following, classified according to their motivation:

1. the young firesetter who sets fires from curiosity or accidentally

2. the cry-for-help firesetter

3. the attention-seeking firesetter

4. the would-be hero firesetter

5. the revenge firesetter

6. the adolescent firesetter who is seeking pleasure or sexual excitement

7. the seriously disturbed (psychotic) firesetter

The younger the child, the more likely it is that firesetting was accidental; among older children, the act of firesetting is not likely to be accidental.

The young, accidental firesetter who plays with matches or lighters sets fires out of curiosity, ignorance, and a desire to experiment. He or she usually has had insufficient parental supervision and can benefit greatly from fire safety or fire prevention education by fire marshals, teachers, parents, or therapists. These children are not intent on causing injury or property damage, and usually pose only a minor risk. Counseling of the parents for the purpose of improving parenting skills is definitely indicated [Webb et al. 1990]. About 15% of our total firesetter group are curiosity firesetters. Such children are referred for firesetter risk evaluations less frequently than others.

An example of a moderate risk for future firesetting is the cry-for-help firesetter who is sending up smoke signals of distress [Macht and Mack 1968]. Here, the firesetting is reactive and is used to obtain help in escaping from an unbearable situation. The emotional needs or claims of these children have not been recognized or responded to by their families, and they are likely to continue to call attention to their emotional distress and suffering by further acts of firesetting. These often dramatic acts are intended to call attention to themselves by frightening, shocking, or antagonizing adults. These troubled children require prompt psychological and psychiatric assessment and therapeutic intervention. Up to 25% of our sample fell into the category of cry-for-help firesetters.

Another, but less common example of firesetting that may be interpreted as attention-seeking behavior is initiated by the child who seeks approval from his role models, especially from firefighters or fire chiefs. About 8% of our sample, most often fatherless boys, set fires to get attention or recognition from firefighters. They will do this by setting a fire, calling it in, and then helping to put out the fire. Once the emotional needs of moderate-risk firesetters are identified and addressed (perhaps by removing the child from a home or foster home where he is being physically, sexually, or psychologically abused), the firesetting usually stops promptly.

A definite-risk firesetter is usually a conduct-disordered, antisocial older child or a delinquent adolescent who is chronically angry and rebellious. This child uses fire repeatedly and maliciously as a primitive weapon in a power struggle with an adult authority whom he or she perceives as depriving, punitive, or rejecting [Yarnell 1940]. At least this is the subjective reality of these children. Generally, they have little superego development or empathy with others, and manifest little or no guilt or remorse over previous episodes of firesetting. In the literature they are sometimes referred to as *pathological firesetters*.

These children or adolescents are often defiant, and the act of firesetting expresses their wish to gain power and triumph over frustrating, depriving, or punishing adults. The firesetting impulse is a response to the impotent rage they feel at lack of control over their lives, or at not getting their way. In effect, the child threatens, "I want my way or I'll destroy something by burning it." They entertain revenge fantasies and are retaliatory in their behavior. Unless intervention is prompt and definite, these juveniles are likely to continue to set fires. Open residential treatment centers are very reluctant to accept such high-risk youngsters into placement, so a specialized or highly structured correctional school would appear to offer the most appropriate placement for them. Some 30% to 40% of our firesetter group have been diagnosed with oppositional disorder or with conduct disorder with strong revenge fantasies.

At extreme risk for future firesetting are children or adolescents belonging to one of two severely disturbed subgroups. They may be adolescent "pyromaniacs," who become sexually or pleasurably aroused or excited by lighting and watching fires burn and develop an irresistible impulse to do so. Their sexual fantasies are associated with firesetting. The act is followed by great relief [Kolko 1989]. (We have seen only one among 180 firesetters who would fit this psychiatric diagnosis. He was included in our severe group, and is described in Appendix A.) David Berkowitz, "the Phantom of the Bronx," was a well-known pyromaniac who set 2,000 fires and turned in 337 false alarms before he was finally apprehended and arrested for murdering young couples in lovers' lanes. However, some 20% of firesetters give evidence of becoming pleasurably aroused or sexually excited in the presence of fires.

Other extreme-risk firesetters were a small number of severely disturbed psychotic children who were seen by us in New York state at Westchester County Medical Center Psychiatric Institute, New York Hospital, and Rockland Children's Psychiatric Center. They were paranoid, lacking in insight and judgment, and responded to command hallucinations, explaining "the devil told me to do it" or "a voice tells me—'light it, light it, light it!'" Because one cannot predict when the devil may tell them to do it again, their behavior must be considered dangerous. Children who constitute an extreme risk require prompt psychiatric hospitalization for the protection of the community and for thorough observation, diagnosis, and treatment.

According to our data, only 6% of the sample fall into the severely disturbed group. These are approximate numbers. Their total exceeds 100% since firesetters often have more than a single motive for their act. Thus, they may be expressing their resentment as well as seeking attention.

Study IV

In an effort to identify and define two important subgroups of firesetters, Studies III and IV both examined individuals classified as either severe or minor firesetters. We hypothesized the presence of certain specific personality characteristics and family background variables that distinguished between the two groups.

In his comprehensive 1980 review of the literature, Fineman wrote, "There is a set or cluster of personality variables that predispose a child toward firesetting, and there is a specific set of circumstances that set the stage for and reinforce the behavior of firesetting." These two studies aimed primarily to identify and highlight the former, the dynamic and behavioral characteristics that predispose a child to act out repeatedly by setting fires. Macht and Mack [1968: 287] first made us fully aware that firesetting behavior is often complex, multidimensional, and overdetermined.

Of the 50 severe firesetters, 46 were male and four were female; of the 50 nonsevere firesetters, 40 were male and ten were female. In age, the serious firesetters ranged from five to 17 and the minor firesetters from seven to 16. The first of these two studies (Study III), entitled "Toward a Clearer Differentiation of High-Risk from Low-Risk Firesetters," was published in *CHILD WELFARE* [Sakheim et al. 1991]. It was a comparison of 25 severe firesetters with 25 minor firesetters. They were compared on 35 qualitative and quantitative variables that have been associated with firesetting or nonfiresetting in the clinical research literature. Since it was published recently, it is not summarized here. The results are quite similar to those of the larger study reported next.

Study IV, Comparison of 50 Minor (Nonsevere) Firesetters with 50 Severe Firesetters, was completed in the summer of 1991. Two-thirds of the 100 children in the sample were either in the residential treatment center or living at the diagnostic center at the time of their evaluation. The remaining third were living at home, in foster homes, in group homes, or at the children's unit of the county psychiatric hospital. These children were referred by the department of social services or the family court after they had set fires. Children from both groups were in all the settings.

Psychological test data, psychiatric evaluations, and social histories of the 100 children were examined for the presence or absence of 35 variables that have been associated with firesetting or nonfiresetting. A complete standard test battery, consisting of the WISC-R, Rorschach, Thematic Appreception Test (TAT), Bender-Gestalt Drawings, and Sentence Completion Test, was used for each subject. Two researchers with advanced training in clinical and developmental psychology rated the data independently for the presence or absence of each study variable. On the few occasions when the two raters disagreed as to the presence or absence of a variable in a record, they discussed the results and the reasons for it, and usually arrived at a conclusion with which both felt comfortable. If disagreement remained (on, for example, whether the child had inadequate superego development, had revenge fantasies, or was defiant), the variable was scored as "absent," because the evidence for its presence was too weak to be convincing. Interrater reliability averaged around 90%.

Chi square statistics were calculated (using Yates' 1973 correction) to compare expected versus actual frequencies in the minor and severe groups for each of the 35 study variables. Differences between the two groups were determined by directional tests consistent with study hypotheses. A stepwise discriminant function analysis [Kerlinger 1973] was then performed, using those variables found to be significantly related to severity of firesetting to derive a prediction equation for group assignment.

The results of Yates' corrected chi-square analyses of the 35 variables indicate that differences exist between the minor and severe groups of firesetters. Statistically significant frequency discrepancies were obtained on 13 out of 35 variables at a probability level of less than .01, and on one variable at a probability level of less than .05. A trend toward statistically significant group differences was found in six variables.

Table 1 summarizes the results of the statistical analyses for all study variables. As shown, inadequate superego functioning, sexual excitement or pleasurable arousal, rage at insults, fantasies of revenge or retaliation, impulsivity, and poor social judgment were all found to be more frequent in the severe than in the minor group, with a high degree of statistical significance ($p<.01$).

Moreover, strong feelings of anger or resentment at maternal rejection, physical or emotional neglect, abandonment or abuse, fire attraction, fire curiosity or preoccupation, sexual conflicts, dysfunction, identity confusion, sexual precocity, and castration anxiety or fear of bodily damage were also found more frequently among the severe than among the minor firesetters, at the .01 level of confidence.

Finally, a lack of empathy with others and the presence of cruelty to children or animals were also found more commonly among the severe than among the minor firesetters. A past history of fire-play characterized 48 out of 50 of the severe group but 40 out of 50 of the minor firesetters. This dif-

Table I. Group Frequency Differences on All Study Variables

Variable	Minor Firesetters (N=50)	Severe Firesetters (N=50)	X Value
Strong feelings of anger at maternal rejection, neglect, abandonment, or abuse	39	49	7.67 **
Strong anger at paternal absence, rejection, abandonment, or abuse	28	36	2.13
Engages in power struggles with adults; is rebellious, oppositional, defiant	31	37	1.15
Fantasies of revenge or retaliation	19	39	14.82 **
Inadequate superego development; lack of morality and decency	14	38	21.19 **
Sexual conflicts or disturbance; identity confusion	26	38	5.25 **
Sexual excitement or pleasurable arousal associated with fires	0	20	22.56 **
Impulsive; poor self-control	38	48	6.73 **
Poor social judgment	19	35	9.06 **
Poor planning or understanding of cause-and-effect relationships	8	17	3.01 trend
Sadistic or destructive fantasies revealed on projective tests or in therapy	41	48	3.68 trend
Rage at insults, disrespect, or humiliation	6	24	13.76 **
Past history of physical violence	37	39	.05
Fire preoccupation, attraction, curiosity, or fantasy; projects fire content	9	30	16.81 **
Wish for reunion with an absent father; to bring him to the rescue	12	8	.56
Past history of fire-play	40	48	4.64 *
Attention-seeking behavior and desire to be a hero	18	15	.18

Continued

Table I (Continued). Group Frequency Differences on All Study Variables

Variable	Minor Firesetters (N=50)	Severe Firesetters (N=50)	X Value
Verbal aggression	35	42	2.03
Feelings of guilt, shame, or remorse re firesetting incident	29	13	11.17 **
Castration anxiety; fear of body damage	28	43	9.52 **
Poor peer relations; feels lonely, isolated, and inadequate	29	35	.84
Obsessive-compulsive traits or defenses	12	7	1.04
Separation anxiety; can form attachments	29	19	3.25 trend
Serious school behavior problems	31	36	.72
Shows cruelty to children or animals	16	34	12.38 **
Lacks empathy with others	25	37	5.14 **
Shows hyperactivity	13	22	2.81 trend
Learning disability present	20	24	.49
History of harsh parental discipline	21	32	3.27 trend
History of little discipline	15	16	0
Limited parental supervision	30	39	3.13 trend
Exposure to fire before age eight	19	28	2.03
Recent life stress; death, divorce, serious illness, new baby	30	30	0
Enuresis	12	16	.54
Diagnosis of conduct disorder	35	38	.20

* p < .05
** p < .01
trend p < .10

George A. Sakheim, Ph.D.
Elizabeth Osborn, Ph.D.
Statistical Analysis: Beverly Richard, Ph.D., Research Consultant

ference is significant at the .05 level. Feelings of guilt, shame, or remorse about the consequences of the firesetting incident, however, were characteristic of the minor firesetters to a much greater extent than was true of severe firesetters (p<.01). Although only 26% of the severe firesetters felt guilty or ashamed of the fires they had set and the destruction they had caused, 59% of the minor firesetters expressed such feelings of guilt or shame. In this respect, the latter group reacted more like normal children who had set a fire by accident and were conscience stricken.

Other interesting trends emerged. Of these, sadistic or destructive fantasies, as revealed on projective tests, and poor planning or poor understanding of cause-effect relationships had been found to be significant variables in two of our earlier studies. A history of limited parental supervision, but harsh parental discipline, and of hyperactivity were new trends that appeared for the first time in the fourth study, which used a larger sample than the others. Finally, separation anxiety and the ability to bond or form attachments were observed more frequently among the minor firesetters.

Study V

In Study V (1992), we combined 55 nonfiresetters with 50 minor firesetters from the previous study, and compared the entire group of 105 nonsevere cases with the 50 severe cases to highlight salient differences between them. Theoretically, we assumed that the minor firesetters (whose firesetting was motivated primarily by curiosity, experimentation, or attention-seeking behavior, or whose fires occurred accidentally), would resemble the nonfiresetters more than the serious or pathological firesetters.

In a second analysis, we compared the same group of 55 nonfiresetters with all 100 firesetters, both severe and nonsevere. The variables that best discriminated the combined group of 100 severe and minor firesetters from the control group of 55 nonfiresetters are depicted in table 2. Only significant results are shown.

The results of Yates' corrected chi-square analysis in study V showed multiple differences between the severe firesetting group and the nonsevere group. Of 36 variables studied, 19 discriminated between the groups at the p<.01 significance level. Three variables yielded trends toward statistical significance (p<.05), and 14 were nonsignificant. Chi-square results are summarized in table 3.

The results corroborated, for the most part, the results of earlier studies. The 19 variables found to differentiate severe from nonsevere firesetters

Table 2. Comparison of 55 Nonfiresetters with 100 Firesetters

Variable	Nonfiresetters	Firesetters	X Value
V-1 Anger at maternal rejection, neglect, or abandonment	12=22%	88=88%	65.03 **
V-2 Anger at father for rejection, abandonment, or abuse	20=36%	64=64%	9.83 **
V-3 Defiant, power struggles, oppositional	9=16%	68=68%	35.8 **
V-4 Fantasies of revenge or retaliation	13=24%	58=58%	15.52 **
V-5 Inadequate superego development	13=24%	52=52%	10.59 **
V-7 Sexual excitement or pleasurable arousal	1=2%	20=20%	8.52 **
V-8 Impulsive; has poor self-control	31=56%	86=86%	15.3 **
V-9 Poor social judgment	7=13%	54=54%	23.6 **
V-11 Preoccupation with sadistic and destructive fantasies	35=64%	89=89%	12.7 **
V-13 History of physical violence	(11/55)=11=20%	76=76%	18.1 **
V-14 Fire attraction, curiosity or fascination	12=22%	39=39%	4.7%**
V-16 History of fire-play	0=0%	88=88%	83.3 **
V-19 Guilt, shame, or remorse about the firesetting incident	N/A	42=42%	
V-22 Obsessive-compulsive traits or defenses	22=40%	19=19%	7.0 **
V-25 Cruelty to children or animals	(3/35)=3=9%	50=50%	16.64 **
V-26 Lack of empathy with others	14=30%	62=62%	12.00 **
V-30 Inadequate parental supervision	(11/34)=11=33%	69=69%	11.75 **
V-31 Exposure to fire before age eight	(1/35)=1=3%	47=47%	20.20 **
V-35 Psychiatric diagnosis of conduct disorder	20=36%	73=73%	18.34 **

** $p < .01$

George A. Sakheim, Ph.D.
Elizabeth Osborn, Ph.D.

had all been found to differentiate other groups, with the same expected directionality, in previous analyses—minors versus majors, or firesetters versus nonfiresetters. The significant variables in the present analysis are generally internal or psychological factors suggestive of a highly negative fantasy life or an angry mood state. Superego/conscience deficits and factors relating to an acting-out psychological profile also appear more frequently in the severe group. The external or behavioral variables that did yield significance are history of fire-play, conduct disorder diagnosis, cruelty to children or animals, limited parental supervision, and exposure to fire at an early age.

Interestingly, these factors are more specific and more directly related to the subject of fire than many of the more global behavioral variables that were not found significant. The variable of guilt or remorse about consequences of match-play or firesetting was found significantly more frequently among nonsevere firesetters, suggesting that this may be a mitigating factor associated with low firesetting risk. Similarly, there was a statistical trend for obsessive-compulsive features to occur more frequently among the nonsevere group than the severe group.

The next analysis involved the construction of a prediction equation from the same database. The chi-square correlational analysis described above demonstrated group frequency differences on independently analyzed variables, but the prediction equation was based on an intrasubject correlational matrix. The prediction equation, therefore, has clinical utility in describing a specific subject's similarity to a particular firesetter research group cage profile on a multiplicity of variables.

Specifically, a stepwise discriminant function analysis [Kerlinger 1973] was performed, using 14 variables found to be significantly related to severity of firesetting to derive a prediction equation for group assignment. The prediction equation is shown in table 4. This equation correctly classified study subjects into the severe or nonsevere firesetting group with 96% accuracy. When data were absent on particular variables, empty cells were set to zero, thereby simulating "real world" clinical conditions. The prediction equation is easily calculated and provides a reliable, valid, and practical method of classifying firesetters as similar to either the severe or nonsevere types.

Both in the five research studies and in our clinical experience, six variables have been found useful to supplement the prediction equation in discriminating between severe or high-risk and minor or low-risk firesetters, as well as between firesetters and nonfiresetters.

Table 3. Comparison of 50 Severe

Variable	Severe	Nonsevere	Chi-Square	Significance
1. Maternal rejection/ emotional deprivation	98.0%	48.6%	34.02	.0000 **
2. Angry w/father for abandonment or abuse	72.0%	45.7%	8.40	.0038 **
3. Defiant of authority; oppositional	74.0%	38.1%	16.06	.0001 **
4. Revenge fantasies	78.0%	30.5%	28.93	.0000 **
5. Poor superego development	76.0%	25.7%	33.14	.0000 **
6. Sexual conflicts	76.0%	51.4%	7.49	.0062 **
7. Sexual excitation or pleasurable arousal	40.0%	1.0%	40.82	.0000 **
8. Impulsivity	96.0%	65.7%	15.19	.0001 **
9. Poor social judgment	70.0%	24.8%	27.18	.0000 **
10. Misunderstood cause and effect	34.0%	16.5%	4.99	.0255 trend
11. WISC PS>VS	60.0%	53.5%	.29	.5873
12. Preoccupation with aggressive fantasies	96.0%	72.4%	10.38	.0013 **
13. Rage at insults or disrespect	48.0%	18.1%	13.66	.0002 **
14. History of out-of-control aggression or violence	78.0%	57.8%	4.75	.0292 trend
15. Attraction to fire; fire curiosity	60.0%	20.0%	22.77	.0000 **
16. Seeks reunion w/father	21.0%	16.0%	.26	.6086
17. History of fire-play	96.0%	47.6%	30.43	.0000 **
18. Attention seeking behavior	30.0%	33.3%	.05	.8171

* $p < .05$
** $p < .01$
trend $p < .10$

versus 105 Nonsevere Firesetters

Variable	Severe	Nonsevere	Chi-Square	Significance
19. Verbal aggression	84.0%	80.0%	.14	.7064
20. Guilt or remorse re firesetting incident	26.0%	58.8%	11.26	.0008 **
21. Fears of body damage	86.0%	66.7%	5.47	.0194 *
22. Loneliness and isolation; poor peer relations	70.0%	55.4%	2.21	.1374
23. Obsessive-compulsive traits	14.0%	32.4%	4.98	.0257 trend
24. Separation anxiety	38.0%	54.3%	2.98	.0847
25. Conduct disorder diagnosis	76.0%	52.4%	6.92	.0085 **
26. Serious behavior problems in school	72.0%	55.4%	2.96	.0853
27. Cruelty to children or animals	69.4%	22.6%	26.32	.0000 **
28. Lack of empathy	74.0%	40.2%	13.77	.0002 **
29. Hyperactivity	44.0%	29.3%	2.36	.1248
30. Enuresis	32.7%	20.5%	1.83	.1763
31. Harsh parental discipline	64.0%	47.5%	2.74	.0979
32. Little parental discipline	32.0%	34.1%	.00	1.0000
33. Limited parental supervision	79.6%	50.6%	9.64	.0019 **
34. Early exposure to fire (before age eight)	56.0%	24.4%	12.08	.0005 **
35. Recent stressful life event	60.0%	56.0%	.08	.7812
36. Learning disability	49.0%	45.8%	.03	.8611

George A. Sakheim, Ph.D.
Elizabeth Osborn, Ph.D.
Statistical Analysis: Beverly Richard, Ph.D., Research Consultant

This is true especially in borderline situations, where the child's score on the prediction equation lies very close to the cutoff score of 0. In these cases, the six additional factors are useful in formulating a clinical assessment of firesetting potential. Their labels are derived from the worksheet that begins chapter 2.

- V-3 The child engages in power struggles for control or domination with adults in authority. The child is often described as rebellious, oppositional, stubborn, challenging authority, or defiant. Although 68% of all 100 firesetters showed defiance, only 16% of nonfiresetters showed this variable.

- V-8 The child is impulsive. He has poor impulse control and there is a temporary breakdown of inhibitions. In this study, 86% of all firesetters and 56% of nonfiresetters demonstrated this variable.

- V-13 The child has a past history of physical violence against persons or destruction of property. Seventy-six percent of all firesetters, but only 33% of nonfiresetters showed this variable.

- V-14 The child is attracted to, curious about, or even fascinated by fire. The child may project fire, explosion, smoke, power, electricity, atom bombs, volcanoes erupting, or other similar images onto the Rorschach or other projectives, or reveal such fantasies or preoccupations during an interview or in therapy. As many as 60% of the 50 severe firesetters revealed the presence of fire attraction, but only 18% of minor or curiosity firesetters and 22% of nonfiresetters did.

- V-19 The child has feelings of guilt, shame, regret, or remorse about the consequences of the specific firesetting incident. Some 58% of the minor or accidental firesetters, but only 26% of the severe or intentional firesetters showed this variable. This variable was not applicable to the group of 55 nonfiresetters.

- V-31 Parental supervision is insufficient or limited. The social history of 33% of the nonfiresetters, 60% of the minor firesetters, but 79% of the major firesetters revealed that they were receiving inadequate parental supervision.

In addition to the 14 variables contained in the prediction equation, these six variables are important to round out the picture of the child who may be difficult to classify into either the severe- or the minor-risk group. Along with the diagnosis of aggressive conduct disorder, these variables help in reaching a diagnostic conclusion about the child.

Statistical Analysis

A stepwise discriminant function analysis [Kerlinger 1973] was performed, using those variables found to be significantly related to severity of firesetting to derive a prediction equation for group assignment.

Table 4. Prediction Equation

	Prediction Equation (Stepwise Discriminant Function)			
Step	Variable	Score	X	Weight
1.	History of playing with fires	(0 or 1)	X	.67
2.	Excitement at fires	(0 or 1)	X	1.36
3.	Revenge fantasies	(0 or 1)	X	.82
4.	Poor social judgment	(0 or 1)	X	.66
5.	Cruelty to animals or people	(0 or 1)	X	1.02
6.	Inadequate superego development	(0 or 1)	X	.65
7.	Fears of bodily harm	(0 or 1)	X	.57
8.	Rage at insults	(0 or 1)	X	.63
9.	Full-scale IQ score	(IQ score)	X	-.01
10.	Severe maternal rejection	(0 or 1)	X	.61
11.	Sexual conflicts	(0 or 1)	X	.49
12.	History of school behavior problems	(0 or 1)	X	-.53
13.	Verbal aggression	(0 or 1)	X	.35
14.	Obsessive-compulsive features	(0 or 1)	X	-.27
			Constant:	-2.63

Interpretation of equation: Score 1 if variable is present; score 0 if variable is absent. Add the products together with the constant. If the result is a negative number, the subject is classified as a minor or low risk for firesetting. If the result is positive, the subject is classified as a definite or severe firesetting risk.

2

Clinical Considerations and Applications

THE WORKSHEET

Following this section is a worksheet for the first step in performing fireset-ter risk evaluations. It defines 25 variables or factors in a child's or adolescent's case record that have been consistently and positively associat-ed with firesetting behavior. The remaining five variables, indicated below, have been associated with nonfiresetting or accidental firesetting behavior, and are considered to be control factors or indicators of ego strength. When present, these five variables diminish the chances that the child will set a serious, destructive fire.

- V-18 Having the ability to verbalize or express feelings of frustration or anger, instead of repressing such feelings and acting them out.
- V-19 Feeling guilt or shame about previous episodes of firesetting.
- V-21 Having obsessive-compulsive traits or defenses.
- V-22 Suffering from separation anxiety.
- V-27 Having empathy with others.

The amount of information gathered in this first step depends on the amount of useful information in the clinical records and other records avail-able or obtainable at the time the child is referred or admitted.

Among the 25 positive predictors of firesetting, 14 make up the prediction equation. These are of primary importance. They are the markers or red flags that help to identify seriously at-risk firesetters. When they appear in a careful study of the child's case record, including a complete social history, a recent psychological evaluation, and a psychiatric examination done with-in the year, they should be coded as 1 and entered into the appropriate space on the worksheet. Although the process is not strictly quantitative, it becomes easy to compute the prediction equation from these data. Addi-tional pertinent information about school and social behavior may be obtained from the child's school report. If the child is hospitalized on a psychiatric ward, information about interpersonal relationships, attitudes, and symptoms may be obtained by reading the nursing notes. Finally, more subtle clues and the child's deeper feelings and attitudes about the firesetting episode(s) may be obtained from a sensitive clinical interview and from specialized supplementary testing, such as the Lowenstein Fire Raising Diagnostic Test [1981].

The Lowenstein, which we regularly administer to help diagnose recurrent firesetting behavior, should supplement the standard battery of clinical psychological tests given to all known and suspected firesetters—WISC-R, Bender-Gestalt, Rorschach, the Thematic Apperception Test (TAT), Sentence Completion, and the House-Tree-Person drawing test (HTP). The Lowenstein consists of 12 questions to be answered true or false by the child. Half of the questions constitute a "lie scale," while the other half relate to firesetting behavior. The lie scale is included to ascertain whether the child is reporting feelings honestly. Some examples: (1) I always do what I'm told to do; (3) I have never and would never steal anything from anyone; (9) Even when nobody is looking, I always do the right thing.

If the subject passes the lie scale, that is, if he does not try to "fake good" or to present himself in a favorable light, then credence can be given to his answers to such fire-related items as (2) I have started fires because I am angry with someone or something; (4) I have found several times [at least twice] that I could not control the spread of a fire I started; (6) I get quite excited when I see a fire burning; and (10) I like playing with fire. Lowenstein states that a "true" answer to questions 6 and 10 is given only by true firesetters, and never by nonfiresetters. We use the Lowenstein as a structured interview, and any affirmative answers to questions 2, 4, 6, 8, and 10 are carefully probed and investigated for additional leads and information.

WORKSHEET FOR PERFORMING A FIRESETTER ANALYSIS TO DETERMINE RISK FACTORS

Clinician: Score one (1) if the variable is clearly present, zero (0) if it is absent, and "Don't Know" if you lack the necessary information to make an informed judgment. (Because of the preponderance of boys among firesetters and for simplicity in reading, the male pronoun is used throughout.)

1. Does this child have strong feelings of anger over maternal rejection, neglect, or abandonment? Does he feel resentment over emotional deprivation, withholding of love and security, or uninvolvement by the mother? _____

2. Is the child disappointed in the father and very angry with him for deserting the family, or for being emotionally distant, unavailable, rejecting, physically or sexually abusive, or for having died and abandoned him? _____

3. Does he try to gain domination or control over adults in the context of a power struggle? Is he hostile, oppositional, threatening, rebellious, or defiant toward authority figures? _____

4. Does he express death wishes or fantasies of revenge against parental figures or peers who he believes have threatened, mistreated, punished, or abandoned him? Does sibling rivalry (resentment of the attention paid to a new baby, or parental favoritism) give rise to jealousy and revenge? _____

5. Does he show weak or inadequate superego development? (lacks morality and decency, steals, lies, cheats, engages in vandalism, sells drugs?) _____

6. Does he manifest marked sexual conflicts, sexual precocity, sexual disturbance, or confusion about his sexual identity? _____

7. Does he become sexually excited, thrilled, or pleasurably aroused by thinking about, by lighting, or by watching fires burn? Is fire used as a sexual substitute? Does he genuinely enjoy setting or watching fires? _____

8. Is he impulsive? Does he act before he thinks? Does he have poor impulse control? Is there a temporary breakdown of inhibitions? _____

9. Does he show poor social judgment (WISC-R Social Comp. score = 7 or less) or is there a psychiatric statement or a social worker's opinion that the child's judgment is poor or impaired? _____

10. Does he misunderstand cause-and-effect relationships, especially in social situations? (WISC-R P.A. score = 7 or less) Does he plan poorly (Mazes = 7 or less)? _____

11. Does he reveal primitive aggressive or sadistic fantasies on projective tests in an interview or in therapy? _____

12. Does he become enraged at insults, teasing, humiliations, or "disrespect" by peers or adults? _____

13. Is there a history of violent or assaultive behavior against persons, or destruction of property? (This variable discriminates between firesetters and nonfiresetters.) _____

14. Is he attracted to, curious about, or fascinated by fires? For example, does he project fires, flames, explosions, smoke, power, electricity, atom bombs, volcanoes erupting, or other such images into the red areas of the Rorschach Test, or does he reveal such preoccupations during an interview or in therapy? (This indicates acting-out of hostility.) _____

15. Is there any history of playing with matches, lighters, or fire? State the number of fire incidents in which this child was involved. _____

16. Has he set fires intentionally, deliberately, "on purpose" (with premeditation)? Did the fires cause serious damage to life or property? _____

17. Is the firesetting a cry for help, to attract attention and to alleviate a stressful or traumatic situation? Is it a distress signal by a physically, sexually, or psychologically abused or exploited child who feels helpless and angry? _____

18. Does he verbalize his frustrations and anger? Does he complain, curse, make demands, or otherwise employ oral aggressive means to ventilate his feelings of dissatisfaction and anger? _____

19. Does he experience feelings of guilt, shame, regret, or remorse about the consequences of his match-play or firesetting? _____

20. Does he have poor peer relations? (Does the child feel lonely, isolated, excluded, and inadequate?) _____

21. Does the child employ obsessive-compulsive traits or defenses to control his impulses? _____

22. Does he suffer from separation anxiety? Can he bond or form attachments? _____

23. Diagnosis: ❏ Aggressive Conduct Disorder
                  ❏ Sociopathic Personality or Antisocial
                     Behavior Disorder
                  ❏ Schizophrenia
                  ❏ Other

24. Does he express fear of bodily harm or mutilation (castration anxiety)? _____

25. Have there been serious behavior problems in school (such as fighting with peers or teachers) leading to suspension or expulsion? _____

26. Has he been known to be cruel to children or to animals? _____

27. Does he lack empathy with others? _____

28. Was he exposed to fire at an early age (before age eight)? (This factor discriminates only between firesetters and nonfiresetters.) _____

29. Is enuresis present? _____

30. Is parental supervision inadequate? _____

31. What is his full-scale IQ? _____

CLASSIFICATION	Minor	Moderate	Definite	Extreme
Firesetting Risk	_____	_____	_____	_____
Not a Firesetting Risk	_____			
Prediction Equation	_____			

George A. Sakheim, Ph.D.
Elizabeth Osborn, Ph.D.

SCORING AIDS

The examples in the following section will aid the reader in scoring the variables that make up the psychological profile of the juvenile firesetter and the prediction equation (table 4 in chapter 1). They illustrate in concrete, specific terms how the variables are scored for presence or absence. Most of the examples were derived from psychological test data such as Rorschach responses, TAT stories, sentence completion items, human figure drawings, and the Lowenstein test. Other examples were drawn from comprehensive social history data, psychiatric examinations, school reports, and psychiatric nursing notes. Every response quoted was given by a firesetter and was scored as 1 (= present) on the worksheet.

1. History of Playing with Matches, Lighters, or Fire

Score 1 if there was at least one previous known firesetting incident in addition to the one that led to the referral.

2. Excitement at Fires

Score 1 if the child or adolescent becomes pleasurably aroused, sexually excited, or turned on by thinking about, lighting, or watching fires. Does he use fire as a sexual substitute?

> Child answers "true" to Lowenstein test item number 6: "I get quite excited when I see a fire burning" (provided "excited" does not mean "scared" or "frightened").

> "When I see the flames it makes me feel good because my anger goes away."

The operative element here is that the child will admit to deriving genuine pleasure from watching, thinking about, or setting fires. This is a serious symptom because we know how extremely difficult it is to give up any pleasurable activity, such as eating, smoking, drinking, or sex.

The following are other examples of pleasurable arousal or sexual excitement drawn from projective test data and from interviews of children and adolescents with a known history of firesetting:

> (Rorschach I): "Two guys fighting over a woman." (Why are they fighting?) "They want her and they are both pulling on her dress."

> (TAT 13MF) "Oh, Oh! He's trying to rape the naked lady (laughs loudly). You can see her things (points). She's still asleep. He just got out of her bed. He killed her—nasty!"

(Rorschach VII): "Two people; they're stuck together." When asked to clarify his answer, he said, "I enjoy lighting fires and seeing the flames."

Another boy told the psychologist that he liked to play with matches.

"I get excited when I see a fire burning because of the glow and the colors; it's fun." (The same boy's Sentence Completion Test): When I see a fire I feel…"Happy." (What makes you feel happy?) "The glow."

From the Sentence Completion Test of a 16-year-old boy who had used a blowtorch to set fire to a neighbor's house "for the fun of it": If something starts to burn…"It starts to smoke up the whole place" (sings out) "Fire, fire—pants on fire!"

Archie, aged 15, came closest to a diagnosis of pyromania among our 180 cases:

"I was born to set fires. My head makes me feel like setting fires." (Archie confessed to lighting one or two fires a week. On a bad day, he lights three or four. If it is a bad week, maybe a big one.) "If I light it and it's too big and I can't stomp it out, I'll call the fire department." "When I light a fire, it's like eating. It's an urge and I get rid of it. After the urge is done with, I'm satisfied for a while." (He then said that he couldn't control himself.) "I don't know why I light fires—that's why I think I'm crazy. I think it's crazy to light fires, but I don't think it's crazy when I light it and watch it." (Later in the interview): "I love it. I enjoy lighting fires. I don't want to stop." (His mother reports that Archie "has been fascinated by fires since he was three years old.") Archie described himself as a "pyromaniac."

A six-year-old who burned down his foster parents' home projected the following onto Card VI of the Rorschach:

"It looks like a snake and the little things stick out…it looks like a stick, sticky, stick, and it's got wings on it; it's a bird…it can't get out the thing…it looks like a fire or something, and here it follows you…and it explodes and goes 'boom!'…it burns the house down." (About this case, the psychologist wrote, "There is the suggestion that the imagery of fire has with it associated sexual tensions.")

A 16-year-old who had set a major, destructive fire in the residential treatment center associated to Rorschach VI (a card weighted for its sexual implications): "It looks like an oil well exploding…an oil well that's just gushed…the oil is coming up and spreading all over the place…like a fountain."

3. Revenge Fantasies

Revenge fantasies may be projected by the child in his associations to the Rorschach, his TAT stories, or his Sentence Completion Test. They may also be confided to a psychiatrist during a psychiatric interview or expressed to a therapist in the course of therapy. Here are some examples taken from case material:

> "When I feel I have been wronged, I sit and think of how I can get even...I think about setting fires, blowing people up, and cutting them with knives."

> "Before I leave PCS, I'm going to burn the cottage down."

> A child tells a TAT story about a man who "wants to get rid of his mother by putting her away."

> A TAT story is about "a woman who kills others as a hobby."

> A boy insisted that the psychiatrist reimburse him for his lost earnings from his job at the swimming pool because he was having a psychiatric interview. When the doctor refused, he threatened to "mess up your telephone if you don't pay me."

> From a psychological report: "Much of M's fantasy life revolves around getting even with others. When M feels he has been done wrong by others, he reacts with passivity, but secretly harbors much resentment and hostility."

In the context of a weak ego structure and attraction to fire, revenge fantasies are a clear danger sign of the potential for deliberately setting a serious fire.

4. Poor Social Judgment

This is indicated when there is a WISC-R social comprehension score of 7 or less (10 is average) or when there is a definite statement in the case record by a psychologist, a psychiatrist, a social worker, or a teacher, preferably backed up by evidence, that in his or her opinion the child's judgment is impaired. Poor social judgment is often associated with other evidence of poor social skills.

5. Cruelty to Animals or People

In the 1990 study, the authors looked for the first time at the tendency to "behave in a cruel or sadistic manner towards other children or animals," which has been reported to be associated with firesetting in the older psychiatric literature. This variable was much more prevalent among serious firesetters or recidivists than among curiosity firesetters. The following are examples from case material:

A boy held his little sister over a highway from an overpass bridge.

A boy stomped on his puppy and broke the puppy's back.

A boy threw a cat into an oil drum at a gas station and then took it to a nearby park and set it on fire.

A boy scalded his younger sister with hot water in the bathtub.

A boy heated a coin on a kitchen stove and then placed it in his little brother's hand.

A boy burned insects alive.

A boy was known for "terrorizing cats."

A girl choked her younger sister and hit her foster brother in the eye; on the Rorschach, the same girl saw Card III as "two birds pulling baby birds out of cracked eggs."

A 13-year-old boy shot another boy in the leg, burned moths alive, shot birds with a BB gun, and chopped up worms.

An eight-year-old "tried to hit his foster parents' younger child with a hammer."

6. Inadequate Superego Development

Score 1 if there is sufficient evidence in the case record or from interviewing and testing the child to conclude that he is lacking in morality and decency. He may have associated symptoms of stealing, lying, cheating, running away from home, habitual truancy, vandalism, prostitution, selling drugs, sneaky, exploitive behavior, and so on. Usually he is lacking in empathy with the victims of his firesetting activities and discusses the incidents in a bland, callous, or indifferent manner. This variable is generally associated with a psychiatric diagnosis of conduct disorder, aggressive type. In this child's TAT stories people usually "get away with murder" or other serious offenses.

7. Fears of Bodily Harm

Score 1 if the child suffers from castration anxiety. He is anxious and concerned about the integrity of his own body. Human figure drawings may have no hands or feet. On the Rorschach, he will project threatening figures such as monsters or giants or anatomical responses.

From a psychiatric evaluation: "The child fears being overpowered and destroyed. He fears retaliation for the expression of his aggression."
From a psychological evaluation: "His fantasies often involve battles between people in which he imagines monsters have been "chopped in half." He sometimes feels like "a fire burning out of control."

A 13-year-old boy told his therapist a dream of being pulled apart by his parents." From another psychological evaluation: "M. experiences the world as a dangerous place where he'll be hurt." (Rorschach III): "It looks like a face that's bleeding...it's been in a gang fight...it looks like blood." (What makes it look like that?) "The eyes are bleeding...blood is dripping from the eyes and the mouth." For Rorschach I, the same child said, "It looks like a fly with cut-up wings; the wings are chewed up here."

8. Rage at Insults, Teasing, Humiliation, or Disrespect from Peers or Adults

This is rage due to wounded narcissism. All examples in this section were given by firesetters.

A child sets fires after being teased by peers and being called a "retard."

A 15-year-old boy's peers teased him repeatedly about his multiple firesetting in the community. They called him "Arsonist!...burn your fingers off. Arsonist!" He became increasingly upset and furious with them and went out and set another abandoned building on fire.

An 11-year-old boy stabbed a girl with a pencil after she had called him a "black nigger."

A 13-year-old girl's stepmother insulted her and her mother, who was chemically dependent. She told her social worker that she could not live with her father and stepmother any longer, and so she set fire to their house.

Another boy was hated and teased by his peers. They called him "Firebug." As a prank, one of them set fire to his shoelaces. After that, he engaged in five to six firesetting episodes during an eight-month period.

A 13-year-old boy shot an older boy in the leg with a BB gun for constantly teasing, humiliating, and tormenting him in front of his girlfriend. "If he got up again, I would have killed him."

"My brother is an asshole, I don't care if he dies." (This was written by a boy who was teased unmercifully by his older brother.)

9. Full-Scale IQ Score

Obtain the full scale IQ score from WISC-R. Multiply it by -.01. Include it in the prediction equation as variable 9.

10. Anger over Severe Maternal Rejection, Neglect, or Abandonment

This variable is scored 1 (or present) when there is clear evidence from the social history, from the child's behavior, from an interview with the child, or from projective test data that he is deeply angry at his mother for rejecting him, neglecting him, or physically or emotionally abusing him. It also includes anger over maternal uninvolvement, distancing, or indifference. The child is left feeling hurt, resentful, and bitter at not being loved or cared for by his mother. In residential treatment centers, such children are sometimes referred to by staff members as "throwaway children."

To allow oneself to experience such anger may be so painful that it is frequently unconscious, repressed, displaced, and acted out. That is, "The child may have to defend against his feelings of rage and sadness around his early abandonment and betrayal and loss" [Webb 1990] and he is left unaware of having any such feelings. Should he be asked about them directly by an interviewer, he may vigorously deny them: "No! It doesn't bother me that my Mom left the family when I was six years old and that she never phones or visits!"

If we, as clinicians, however, know that certain traumatic events have taken place in a child's life, or can infer from the history that anger at maternal rejection, neglect, or abandonment must be present and would be entirely natural and appropriate in the situation (if most children, when placed in such a situation, would feel intensely hurt, sad, and angry with their mothers), but the child who is being evaluated does not seem to feel or acknowledge it, he may be defending against such painful feelings, and we score the variable as present, even though the child may deny that he has such feelings.

Examples of maternal rejection:

A drug-addicted mother never visits her son in the residential treatment center; she neglected him before he went into placement; she consistently breaks appointments with his social worker.

The TAT story is, "He put his wife in the cellar and she died."

A boy has engaged in physical fights with his mother, has twisted her arm, and has often defied her authority; he is argumentative and talks back to his teachers.

From his psychiatric evaluation: "This child has received minimal nurturing...he feels unattended, neglected, and unloved...unconsciously, he feels very angry with her...he runs away from home and sets fires."

This girl has strong feelings of anger at having been physically abused by both parents and sexually abused by her stepfather in the mother's absence. She has been diagnosed as suffering from "maternal deprivation."

Rorschach VII response given by a boy: "A girl turns into a monster."

The following striking example is taken from a social history and from psychological testing:

"M. was an unplanned and unwanted baby, born during a period of marital strife. He was delivered by Caesarean section after 16 hours of labor." The social worker describes the mother as "uncomfortable with her son. She attempts to avoid interaction with him. She is detached and expresses little interest in him." M. experiences his mother as distant, uncaring, and rejecting, and feels that she favors his sister. He has set several fires to the family home. On the psychological exam, he told the following story about a picture of a boy falling down a flight of stairs with a concerned looking woman standing nearby: "I broke both of my legs and you, bitch, knocked me down the stairs."

11. Sexual Conflicts, Sexual Disturbance, Sexual Precocity, or Identity Confusion
Examples:

A 12-year-old boy touched his sister and grandmother inappropriately.

From a report about a ten-year-old boy whose mother is a prostitute: "He frequently watched his mother have sexual intercourse with her clients and saw her shoot and kill one of them. At age nine, this boy is described as sexually preoccupied; he has a girlfriend and buys her clothing and jewelry.

Another nine-year-old boy molested a six-year-old boy in his foster home.

From a school report: "This eight-year-old shows inappropriate sexual preoccupation in school, including telling sexual jokes and pretending he is carrying around a penis."

A 14-year-old girl claimed to be pregnant (she wasn't), and was eating for two; she also engaged in sex play with her three-year-old brother.

At age nine, a boy "sexually fondled" his two younger sisters; "he did nasty things to them."

At age 11, a boy still wants to sleep with his mother and be her "protector."

A 14-year-old boy was sexually abused at the age of three by his drug-addicted mother and her boyfriend; later on, he molested several of his adoptive siblings.

12. A History of School Behavior Problems Leading to Suspension or Expulsion

Examples:

A child threw a chair at his teacher.

A 13-year-old girl was removed from class for frequent disruptive behavior.

A boy has a long history of aggressive behavior at school, including disrespect toward the teacher, fighting with peers, making strange noises, and running out of the classroom; he also continually threatened to burn the school down.

A boy physically assaulted a teaching assistant.

A boy states that he is being harassed in school, makes graffiti, and fights on the school bus.

A boy was referred to the school psychologist for "bizarre behavior" and uncontrolled emotional reactions: "He was often disruptive in class and got into numerous fights with peers."

A boy fought with a rival for his girlfriend; a boy with chronic truancy and hyperactivity was suspended; he was also assaultive to peers and started fires.

13. Verbal Aggression

The child verbalizes his frustrations and anger. He complains, curses, is verbally demanding, or otherwise employs "oral-aggressive" means to express his feelings of dissatisfaction and anger.

For example, he projects oral-aggressive themes or animals on the Rorschach: (Card II): "two birds fightin'…they look like they're mad…their beaks are open and they look like they're screamin'." (Card VIII): "Two wolves, two wild animals…an animal about to attack." (Card V): "A vampire bat who bites." (Card VI): "A dragon monster who eats people."

A child projects oral-aggressive animals such as foxes, lions, rats, termites, crabs, spiders, cougars, or jaguars.

A child draws a shark about to devour a person, based on the movie *Jaws;* a boy draws a human figure showing prominent teeth.

A 16-year-old boy escaped from a cult of which his father was an abusive member; he wrote to his father from a residential treatment center, "I hate you. I will smash your head, tear your heart out and eat it."

A boy is very demanding and "argumentative with his mother."

At age nine, a boy used obscene language against his aunt and uncle; later, he set their house on fire.

A child is verbally very abusive to the hospital staff on the ward.

In school, a boy was described as "defiant, cursed at the teacher, and had to be removed; he also constantly verbalized his desire to do harm to peers, adults, and animals."

14. Obsessive-Compulsive Traits or Defenses

There is ample evidence in the case record or in the child's interaction with the psychologist of obsessive-compulsive ideation, defenses, or behavior.

From a psychological report, "M. is rigidly compulsive; his overall style of functioning is highly orderly, methodical, and painfully exact."

From a psychiatric evaluation: "His great rage is sometimes bound by obsessive-compulsive mechanisms, but frequently it bursts forth in a hostile, sometimes dangerous act."

A 14-year-old boy tells very detailed and elaborate TAT stories, and drew his human figure drawings showing the most minute and elaborate details.

A 16-year-old girl has obsessional thoughts and compulsive rituals; from a psychological exam: "The figure drawings were large and expansive, with an elaboration of details and embellishment that suggests both obsessiveness and fantasy activity."

A 16-year-old boy with obsessive defenses "worries a great deal about wasting time"; from another psychological report: "His obsessive defenses and constricted style of functioning are often not successful in containing his pressing needs."

Firesetting has also been consistently associated in the literature with DSM-III-R diagnoses of both the aggressive and the nonaggressive subtypes of conduct disorder.

In addition, fire curiosity, fascination, or attraction to fire are revealed on projective tests by two or more fire associations, such as volcano, rocket, electricity, bomb, or explosion responses; or on the TAT or the House-Tree-Person test. This variable was three times as frequent among the recidivists (60%) as among accidental firesetters (18%). Here are some examples taken from our case material:

> An association to Rorschach Card VII—"It looks like smoke and some people made a fire…they took a match and lit it."

> An association to Rorschach Card IV—"A gremlin jumping over a johnny-pot (a fire hydrant)."

> Rorschach X—"A spider carrying a torch."
> Rorschach X—"The head of a monster with firecrackers exploding all round him."

> From a Sentence Completion Test—"He drew back from the…flames." "If people only knew how much…fire is in the world."

> Rorschach VII—"Two Indian boys carrying a sack of smoke."

> Rorschach IX—"Two dragons spitting fire at each other."

> Rorschach VI—"It looks like a flame up here…a star…a gun…with handles…a machine gun…a sword…one last thing…a bow and arrow."

> One seven-year-old boy associated fire to the phallic area on Card VI, followed by some very aggressive, warlike imagery; this boy had made a pile of his older sister's clothes and set fire to it.

The remaining 11 variables listed on the worksheet that are not included in the prediction equation, such as V-3 (engages in power struggles; defiant, oppositional), V-10 (poor planning or understanding of cause and effect relationships), and V-14 (fire-attraction, curiosity, or preoccupation), when present, add important information to the process of determining whether we are dealing with a definite firesetting risk. In the clinical and research literature, these variables or dynamics have been proposed repeatedly as codeterminants associated with firesetting. They were found to be correlated with firesetting tendencies in at least three out of five of our research studies. They should help in fleshing out the picture and arriving at a firm conclusion about the degree of risk for recidivism a particular child presents.

THE INTERVIEW

To gain a deeper understanding of the child's motivation or purpose in starting a fire, a probing interview is focused on the circumstances surrounding the fire. Why did the child set the fire at the particular time he did? Here it is important to remember that most firesetters have conduct disorders and will usually minimize or deny involvement in the firesetting. Most often, they project the blame onto siblings or peers. Therefore, when investigating a fire in the school, at home, or in the neighborhood, one has to be something of a detective. It is advisable not to take the first or even the second "No, I didn't do it" for an answer. Take the time necessary to explore further.

Questions such as the following are useful and pertinent:
1. Have any of your friends ever started a fire?
2. Have you ever played with matches or lighters, or started a fire?
3. What did you set on fire?
4. What did you use for making the fire?
5. How many fires have you set? (Get details.)
6. Where were they? (Inside the home? Outside? In school?)
7. Did anything important happen to you before the fire?
8. What were you thinking before the fire?
9. How did you feel just before you made the fire?
10. How did you feel when you saw the flames?
11. What did you do right after the fire? (Examples: try to put it out, tell someone or call for help, stand and watch it burn, or run away).
12. Who put the fire out? (You? Your parents? Did the fire department have to be called?) The child's behavior right after the fire is very important from a prognostic point of view.
13. Did you get punished for having set the fire? What was the punishment? Did you think it was fair?
14. Now that it's all over and behind you, how do you feel about having set the fire? (Is there any genuine shame, guilt, remorse, or embarrassment, or is there only blandness, nonchalance, indifference, or annoyance at being apprehended?)

THE PROGNOSIS FOR RECIDIVISM

In assessing the probability of a given child becoming a recidivist, we look at base rates for all juvenile firesetters. In examining these base rates, however, we bear in mind that "there is a high prevalence of fire-play even in normal children" [Grolnick et al. 1990]. According to these authors, "More than one-third of their sample of 770 six to 14 year old school children had at some point played with fire, and 14% reported having played with fire within the previous six months."

Stewart and Culver [1982] found that seven out of 30 children hospitalized in a psychiatric hospital for firesetting were continuing to set fires three years after they were discharged from the hospital. Thus, in their study, about one firesetter in four turned out to be a recidivist. These recidivists are described by the authors as "more antisocial, less conforming, and more deviant" than children who had stopped setting fires. Jacobson [1985] found one in five firesetters to be "dangerous"—children who were sufficiently disturbed and acting out to merit hospitalization.

After reviewing the literature dealing with the frequency of firesetting behavior, Kolko [1985] concluded that "children who set one fire will probably set additional fires. Clearly, greater attention should be paid to the frequency of previous firesetting incidents." In a 1992 publication, Kolko and Kazdin investigated the important issue of recidivism among firesetters. Their retrospective data indicate that as many as 52% of child-outpatient and 72% of inpatient firesetters had set a second fire within a 12-month period. "Recidivists were rated by their parents as more antisocial and noncompliant, and they resided more often [than other children] with psychiatrically disturbed parents."

Using parent and child interviews in the same study, and employing a sample of 138 firesetters and nonfiresetters between the ages of six and 13, Kolko and Kazdin found that "of 78 children who were initially classified as nonfiresetters, 14 (or 18%) later had set a fire. Of 60 children initially identified as firesetters, 21 (or 35%) had set an additional fire by follow-up." In this study, recidivism was associated with children's greater than average knowledge about things that burn and with involvement in fire-related activities. There were also more community complaints about fire-play, hostility, and carelessness on the part of the children, lax parental discipline, and family conflict and disorganization. The recidivists acknowledged more maternal rejection than nonrecidivists, and a heightened attraction to fire.

Because recidivism rates for firesetters reported in the literature are high, ranging from 23% to 72%, it is imperative in the initial assessment of a newly referred firesetter to assess whether he fits the psychological profile of the severe or of the nonsevere firesetter. It is at this point in the process of evaluation that the prediction equation can help greatly to arrive at an accurate assessment of firesetting risk.

It is essential to understand the child's motivation for setting the fire. What was his intention or his purpose in lighting the fire? What, if any, sexual, aggressive, magical, or omnipotent fantasies were associated with lighting the fire? What results did it achieve for him? Did fire symbolize something special for him, such as sending up a warning or smoke signals? Has the child learned anything from this experience? What is his attitude toward the fire now, as he looks back on it? Has he learned to fear and respect fire?

One must also look closely at a child's behavior right after the fire. *The Psychology of Child Firesetting* by Gaynor and Hatcher [1987] features a useful table dealing with how the child acts right after he sets a fire: Does he become frightened by what he did and try his best to put it out? Does he call for help or run in search of adults to obtain help? Does he stand there and watch it burn? Or does he run away and let it burn, not telling anybody about it? Each of these actions carries different prognostic implications. By employing data derived from several sources, such as a detailed family history, behavioral observations, school reports, a focused clinical interview, and the results of projective personality tests, we are able to extrapolate both the conscious and the unconscious determinants of firesetting in any individual case. This results in a well-rounded, in-depth understanding of the young firesetter's motivation for his antisocial act. The child-environment interaction is another important variable that must be considered when assessing the degree of risk for recidivism, which may be either increased or decreased depending on the environment in which the child is located.

In the same publication, Gaynor and Hatcher discuss individual characteristics of child firesetters. They point out that "there is some clinical evidence suggesting that the [child's] underlying emotional state and ability to express experienced emotions may be related to recurrent pathological acts of firesetting." Addressing the psychodynamics of pathological firesetting, they write:

> Youngsters involved in repeated firestarts are primarily experiencing overwhelming feelings of aggression and anger. Because they lack both the ability to understand the reasons for their anger as well as the skill to appropriately express their feelings, they chose firesetting as a means of displaying their aggression. Although the link between multiple firestarts and emotional state and expression has been clinically observed, confirmation from empirically based investigations is necessary to verify this interpretation of recurrent firesetting behavior. There is an apparent relationship between the emotional state and expression of youthful firesetters and the motivations underlying their behavior. Although there appear to be a number of different rea-

sons for repeated firesetting, the common theme of these intentions seems to be that recurrent firesetting is an expression of internal conflict and emotional turmoil. The firestarts themselves may represent emotional discharges of displaced revenge or nonspecific anger. In addition, it has been suggested that firesetting indicates a need for recognition and attention with some clinical reports indicating [that] recurrent firesetters have strong desires to be perceived as heroes. [Gaynor and Hatcher 1987:77]

The reader will find considerable congruence between the individual characteristics Gaynor and Hatcher associate with serious firesetting and the results of our research studies of severe firesetting. If, for example, after a period of psychiatric hospitalization, a cry-for-help firesetter is returned to the same rejecting, depriving, or abusive home or foster home that he tried to set on fire before the hospitalization, it should come as no surprise to anyone if in due course, after the immediate beneficial effects of the nurturance and tight structure of hospitalization have dissipated, the child should set another fire.

If the parents or foster parents, however, receive counseling, both during and after their child's hospitalization, which deepens their understanding of the child's needs and enhances their parenting skills, the risk level may be greatly reduced. If such a course has already been tried, or is not feasible due to the child's or parents' psychopathology, the risk level may also be reduced by placing the emotionally disturbed youngster in a neutral setting such as a residential treatment center. There he would receive the nurturance, the structure, the supervision, and the good adult role models he needs to foster his development and to bring his firesetting impulses under control.

This work has endeavored to better forecast future firesetting behavior in children and adolescents. If an old axiom in psychology, that "the best predictor of future behavior is past behavior," were altogether true, we would have to assume that a child who has already set several fires would continue setting fires indefinitely. This is obviously a shaky conclusion. It fails to take into account the child's ability to learn from his experience, as well as from any number of planned therapeutic interventions, including fire-safety education, counseling or psychotherapy, removal from home, placement in a therapeutic setting, or the effect and influence of other variables, both facilitating and inhibiting, included in this study.

In summary, we have developed a worksheet, a prediction equation, and an interview as guides to aid the clinician in evaluating children who are suspected firesetters. These instruments developed in the course of our five research studies can enhance the clinician's ability to assess and classify a suspected firesetter and to make a prognosis for recidivism.

In the process of arriving at a firm conclusion as to whether a particular child is best classified as a minor, moderate, definite, or extreme risk for future firesetting in the community, all available clinical and research findings are integrated. Clinical data and validated research data obtained from the literature usually support each other, but on occasion there are contradictions. In our experience in such situations, there is no substitute for sound, critical clinical judgment. When doubt persists, however, we tend to give priority to well-established and accepted research findings.

This drawing and the four that follow are the work of severe or major firesetters, in response to the psychologist's standard request to "please draw a house, a tree, and a person."

1. The child on the scooter (lower right) stands between the speeding police car, with its flashing lights and blaring horn, and the house on fire around the corner.

II. Note the meticulous execution of the large chimney structure, with smoke emerging from the top of the chimney.

III. Note the unusual fire escape drawn on the wall of the house, as well as the street light burning like a sun.

IV. A drawing of a house that is clearly on fire.

V. Drawn in response to "please draw a man."
Note the prominent burning cigarette.

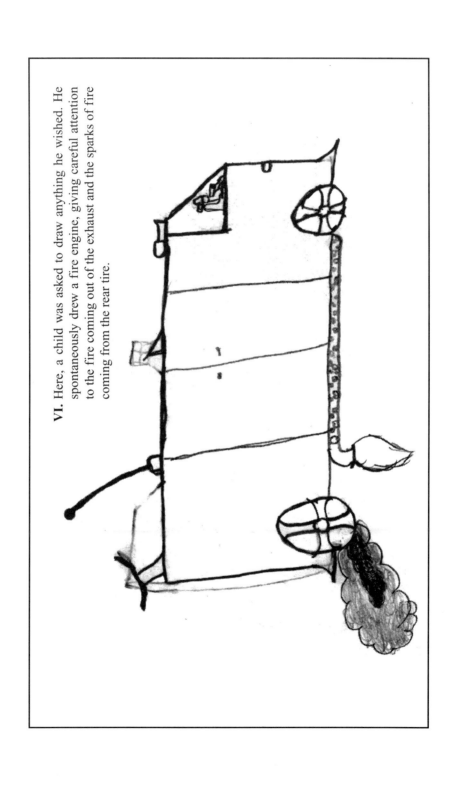

VI. Here, a child was asked to draw anything he wished. He spontaneously drew a fire engine, giving careful attention to the fire coming out of the exhaust and the sparks of fire coming from the rear tire.

3

Recommendations for Treatment and Placement

The assessment of the level of firesetting risk should lead to specific recommendations for treatment or placement. Although there may be some overlap, cases can usually be classified into one of four categories: little risk, moderate risk, definite risk, and extreme risk. Some effective approaches to the management and treatment of minor- or little-risk, moderate-risk, definite-risk, and extreme-risk firesetters were suggested earlier during the definition and discussion of the four subgroups.

It is the consensus in the literature that minor-risk or little-risk, curiosity, or accidental firesetters benefit the most from educating the parents and child in the home and improving parental supervision. This is usually accomplished with the aid of the local fire department's fire safety education program or the child's local school system's fire prevention program. The more children are exposed to good fire safety education, the less likely they are to experiment with matches or lighters.

In our experience, minor- and moderate-risk firesetters may be treated in the community, provided that such safeguards as close parental supervision of the child, counseling or psychotherapy for both child and parents, and sound fire safety education are built into the treatment program, and provided that the child and parents keep their appointments with their therapist or clinic [Webb et al. 1990]. In psychotherapy, these children need skilled professional help to identify and label their feelings and to find more adaptive ways of expressing feelings than setting fires. More specifically, they need to learn socially appropriate expressions of their burning resentment, anger, or jealousy without resorting to acting out by firesetting. It should be remembered that the firesetting of the moderate-risk, cry-for-help firesetter is most often reactive to a very stressful or intolerable situation. It is an important symbolic communication to the family that the child cannot handle a particular situation, whether it is family discord, a separation, parental divorce, a physically or sexually abusive home or foster home, or an open residential setting.

In a clear and concise statement, Gaynor and Hatcher [1987: 16] describe how minor-risk, definite-risk, and extreme-risk cases may be managed.

> For those children classified as minor risk, an educational approach has been shown to be the most effective in reducing future firesetting involvement. For definite-risk children, a complete psychosocial evaluation is recommended, accompanied by one or more interventions such as counseling, psychotherapy, or help from community services to meet the individual needs of the youngsters and their families. Extreme-risk cases, although occurring relatively infrequently, not only require a complete psychosocial assessment, but also necessitate long-term intensive inpatient or residential treatment. This typology of intervention strategies represents general treatment recommendations that are used in conjunction with the system of risk-level classification for youthful firesetters.

In a single case study of a $12^1/_2$-year-old, female, moderate-risk firesetter, "A Female Firesetter: A Case Report" [Awad and Harrison 1976], psychoanalytically oriented psychotherapy combined with marital and family therapy were the modes of treatment. After having set two previous fires, Mary set fire to the dining room drapes while her mother was having a drink with her employer on the porch of the family home. Looking for determinants of the symptom choice in this girl, the authors point to the fact that she knew of her parents' imminent divorce and of the suspected romantic liaison between the mother and the boss. They felt her firesetting "was an acting out of an aggressive impulse directed at her mother and the mother's boss" that broke through controls, a hidden wish to hurt the mother, or a desperate cry for help. Because of a rigid family style, the initial assessment led to a poor prognosis. However, the fact that Mary's firesetting was not ego-syntonic was hopeful. Therapy brought about some changes in the family situation and demonstrated a "general improvement in the girl's ego functioning, enabling her to recognize and express anger more appropriately rather than automatically controlling it and expressing it more impulsively." Her attitude toward firesetting changed, and she had a good prognosis for the cessation of firesetting.

A 1972 paper by Richard Eisler, "Crisis Intervention in the Family of a Firesetter," describes short-term innovative and effective family therapy techniques in the treatment of a 14-year-old male moderate-risk (cry-for-help) firesetter who had set several large grass fires. It was Eisler's intention to show the utility of viewing an individual's deviant behavior as representative of disturbed social (family) relationships, and to suggest that treatment should focus on the social relationships rather than on the disturbed behavior of the individual who is the designated patient. The therapist concluded that the boy's firesetting was a complex, rather desperate nonverbal communication to the family. The problem was resolved during seven two-to-three hour sessions with the entire family. One year after the termination, no further incidents of firesetting had taken place, and the family was functioning much better.

From an interpersonal analytic point of view, Macht and Mack [1968] describe and clarify the psychodynamics and psychotherapy of four adolescent firesetters classified in the cry-for-help yet definite-risk category. It is an in-depth case study that provides a wealth of relevant and interesting information about these four cases. Macht and Mack emphasize the meaning and purpose of the firesetting behavior in each adolescent's psychic life. It is of interest that in all four cases, the father had some significant involvement with fires but was absent from home when the fires were set. The authors describe the "associated behaviors and fantasies that accompany the firesetting. ...These include turning in the alarm, waiting for the firemen to arrive, watching and assisting in the extinguishing operation, establishing a relationship with the firemen, using firesetting as a signal to obtain help, and expressing intense sexual excitement and destructive wishes and impulses throughout the firesetting behavior." The authors show that "setting fires is a highly determined behavioral complex or syndrome with important instinctual, defensive, and adaptive aspects."

Bumpass et al. [1983] developed a graphing technique for children who have set fires on purpose (definite risk). The child is taught to pay attention to and correlate his feelings, his mood, and his thoughts just before the firesetting incident. The authors conceptualize the incident as the culmination or triggering event of an emotional chain reaction consisting of brief but intense feelings of sadness, loneliness, boredom, restlessness, anger, and rage. The child gets a match or lighter, strikes it, and sets a fire. Some children cannot handle uncomfortable emotions and tend to find some mechanism for discharging their feelings rapidly. The graphing technique helps children to understand why they set fires by showing them the connection between their feelings and their firesetting behavior. In effect, it teaches them the cause and effect relationship between their strong negative feelings and their behavior.

Behavioral treatment techniques were used by R.S. Welsh [1971] to help bring firesetting under control in curiosity or minor-risk firesetters. As reported by Vreeland and Levin in 1980,

He used stimulus satiation to eliminate firesetting behavior in two-to-seven-year-old boys. Each child was given the opportunity to strike as many matches as he wished, one by one, for one hour each day. This procedure was carried out in the therapist's playroom under the supervision of the therapist. In one case, the child was required to hold each match until he felt the heat on his fingertips and then to blow it out; in the other case, each match was to be held over the ashtray at arm's length until most of the match had burned, without allowing the extended arm to be supported on the table or by the other arm. When the child asked to stop lighting matches, he was requested to light a few more matches in the same manner and then allowed to engage in some play activities. Firesetting was eliminated in both the playroom and in the home in just a few sessions. The parents reported that at home the boy no longer seemed fascinated with fire play. Follow-up over the next six months or so revealed no recurrence of firesetting behavior in the home.

The eminent child psychiatrist Stella Chess notes [1978: 128–129]:

Firesetting cannot be assessed solely on the basis of its obvious danger. It is the study of the particular child or adolescent who has set the fire that can unravel the significance of the act and the possibility of its future repetition. When the firesetter is a timid, withdrawn child, he must be helped to feel less isolated and to participate in gratifying relationships with his peers. Aggressive, hostile children are in need of close supervision and structure in their activities in order to find more constructive avenues for the expression of their feelings. Depressed, inadequate adolescents are most responsive to efforts that provide them with means of bolstering their self-esteem. Children who are fascinated with fire can be helped to find more appropriate ways of being associated with fire without endangering their community.

In this connection, Fineman writes [1980: 495] that "the most effective intervention for both curiosity firesetters and pathological firesetters involves education about fire during their formative years." Emphasizing the importance of working with firesetters' parents to improve their parenting skills, Fineman cites the work of Vandersall and Weiner [1970]. They suggest that "therapy [should] meet the child's dependency needs to give him control over his aggression, even if this means inpatient treatment." Siegelman and Folkman [1971] suggest that therapy helps the child achieve a sense of mastery through learning the appropriate use of fire. However, the authors stress the need for more than the suppression of firesetting behavior, cautioning against an approach that teaches about "the fire without," while at the same time ignoring "the fire within." In our opinion, also, behavioral techniques that address only the overt symptom of firesetting miss the dynamic significance that firesetting has for many children—a shortcoming of these techniques.

A child who has set fires while living at home and who is the product of a seriously disturbed and dysfunctional family cannot be relieved of his underlying tensions merely by being separated from his parents and placed in a foster home. The newly introduced separation anxiety he experiences may activate continuing stimuli to the underlying impulse, and firesetting may reappear in a revitalized form. It often becomes necessary to place such a damaged child for a period of time in the more neutral atmosphere of a residential treatment center for structure, treatment, and rehabilitation [Nichtern 1984].

Although residential treatment centers may be reluctant to accept potentially dangerous children for treatment and rehabilitation, definite-risk firesetters require the structure, supervision, healthy adult role models, psychotherapy, and often the special education that only a well-run residential treatment center can provide. If a child is truly a definite risk according to our criteria, is fascinated by fires, shows no guilt about previous acts of firesetting, has a conduct disorder, and does not have a genuine interest in bringing this dangerous behavior under control, he should not be allowed to remain in the community. Sooner or later, he is likely to set another destructive fire. Whether to place such a child in an institution is a judgment call, not only for the consultant, but also for the entire professional team already involved with the case and for the child's parents. Sometimes, of course, the law is involved as well, and after hearing the police, lawyers, and mental health professionals, it is the judge who makes the final decision about placement.

The field is greatly indebted to Lowenstein [1981] for a model of an inpatient program for definite-risk firesetters. Lowenstein has treated severe firesetters in a specially designed therapeutic community school, Allington Manor, near Southhampton, south of London. He writes that "the goal of the therapeutic community is to treat the child and protect him from his own inclinations, as well as to protect the outside world from the destructive forces of arson."

Lowenstein has described his comprehensive treatment program in a personal communication and in a privately circulated paper, "The Diagnosis and Treatment of Child and Adolescent Arsonists by a Combination of Treatment Approaches in a Therapeutic Community." The program consists of the following elements: (1) establishing a diagnosis of firesetting behavior; (2) redirecting hostile and destructive impulses; (3) dealing with the total conduct disorder syndrome within a therapeutic milieu providing adequate supervision and control; (4) providing consistent security; (5) never rejecting a child regardless of the behavior he often manifests, which would ultimately result in rejection by his family or a treatment center; (6) redirecting pleasure or enjoyment in a direction other than firesetting; (7) developing a more adequate person by promoting self-esteem; (8) helping the child to become aware of his desire to retaliate against rejecting parents; (9) providing alternatives to firesetting behavior as outlets for anger, dissatisfaction, revenge, frustration, and so on; (10) promoting identification with an adult role model of good standards and values; (11) promoting the development of self-control over his negative emotions and behavior. Seven additional components of this treatment program are not included in the interest of brevity.

Out of nine adolescents, ages 14 to 16, who completed his program of from one to three years, "Three resumed their firesetting behavior and in due course received custodial and secure-type placements. These three tended to be older children whose problems had hardened into habitual behavior, difficult to reverse. ...Early detection and treatment at a younger level might well prevent long periods of incarceration due to firesetting behavior or the threat of it." Lowenstein stresses that "the treatment of the rejection syndrome of such children is very difficult since it occurs very often at an early stage in their lives, hence makes a lasting impression on them."

Extreme-risk firesetters are usually psychotic or sociopathic children or adolescents, or pyromaniacs. They are almost always evaluated in a psychiatric hospital setting. They usually face a prolonged period of hospitalization while their pathological and persistent firesetting tendencies are treated by the staff. When they are no longer actively psychotic and the staff considers them ready for discharge, unless there has been a dramatic improvement or turnaround enabling return to the community, they should be referred to a highly structured facility or correctional school for long-term care. In this setting they can learn to improve their social skills, raise their self-esteem, and bring their violent acting-out behavior under control.

4

Case Example of a Severe Firesetter

The worksheet reproduced in chapter 2 presents and summarizes the relevant dynamics of a specific case. To illustrate its application, we shall use as an example a case that was seen recently in consultation by one of the authors, Dr. Sakheim. On the adolescent unit at a psychiatric hospital in New York state, I saw a 15-year-old hearing-impaired Caucasian boy, Steven, who had set seven fires involving empty buildings and a house trailer with his stepfather, a volunteer fireman, as well as five fires by himself. Soon after the stepfather married Steven's mother, he began to sexually abuse Steven, then nine years old, on a regular basis, and taught him and encouraged him to set fires. By a combination of threats and bribes, the stepfather forced Steven to set fires even when he did not want to. Steven reported later that he felt "nervous and scared" during the fires. At the age of 14, Steven was finally caught and arrested by the New York State Police. At the police station, he confessed the whole story to the detectives. The boy's mother, who was working outside the home throughout this period, did not know what was happening because most of the abuse took place on "fishing trips" the stepfather took Steven on—usually right after they had set a fire.

The stepfather was promptly arrested and interrogated, confessed, was tried, and was sentenced to one to three years in jail for sodomy. Steven's mother divorced him. When Steven was asked, during my interview with him, why he did not tell his mother about the abuse, he said, "She wouldn't have believed me. She would have yelled at me. She would have believed John." The stepfather had also threatened to beat Steven or hurt his cat if he ever told anyone. Though Steven's biological father lived in the same community with his new family, he had shown very little interest in Steven since the boy was six, when the parents were divorced.

Steven explained to his social worker that he set the five fires alone, and closer and closer to his home, "to tell my mom that something was wrong—that I was being abused." He also told her that he told his stepfather about the fires he set alone because "I hoped he would stop teaching me [and molesting him] if he saw that I could set them alone." After the stepfather's arrest, the mother finally got the message and began to pay more attention to her son. She visited him regularly at the hospital where Steven was receiving individual and group therapy to deal with the sexual abuse and the firesetting. He was making a good adjustment, was cooperative and friendly, and was well liked by the staff. He was on the behavior modification "A level" and had privileges. He had shown no interest in matches or fires. However, since it was highly probable that no residential treatment center would accept him with his serious firesetting history [Fine and Louie 1979: 435], his mother reluctantly agreed to take him home to live with her. Steven was disgusted with the light sentence his stepfather received. When asked what sentence he would have given the stepfather if he were the judge, Steven said, "Fifteen years; they didn't even count the fires." He said that he was happy the man was in jail, and that he (Steven) did not miss him.

On the worksheet, Steven was given positive scores for the following variables that have been identified as positive predictors of child/adolescent firesetting in the research and clinical literature:

V-1 Intense anger at maternal neglect, distancing, and emotional deprivation. For example, for a drawing of a female, he drew a large pouting woman in profile, without any ears and with only minimal eyes. When asked what she was doing, he said, "She is looking in a different direction." Thus, she was paying no attention to him.

V-2 Anger at paternal unavailability, indifference, and abandonment by the biological father at age 10, and long-standing coercive sexual abuse by the stepfather. The psychologist who tested him soon after his admission to the hospital wrote, "His rationale behind lighting fires related to feelings of anger and disappointment in his caregivers." The examining psychiatrist wrote, "His relationship with his mother is obviously distant. She is indifferent to him, and told the doctor, 'I don't want him to be a menace. I can't be responsible for him.'" By his firesetting, Steven also expressed his need to call attention to himself. Steven did not receive the emotional supplies needed for survival from either parent, and neither parent was there for him to protect him from the abuser.

V-4 Revenge fantasies directed against the abuser. "One to three years is not enough; he should have received 15 years." Also, for a male human figure drawing, he drew a powerfully built and malevolent looking "spider-man" with clenched fists and large boots. He accentuated both the eyes and the ears. As Steven described him, "He likes to fight, and he is the Avenger."

V-6 Sexual conflicts, sexual precocity, and sexual identity confusion. The stepfather initiated him into oral and anal sexual practices by first tying him to his bed.

V-8 Impulsivity.

V-9 Poor social judgment. He accepted sexual abuse for five years without telling his mother, his grandmother, whom he loved, or his teacher.

V-11 Aggressive and sexual fantasies were fused on projective tests. The phallic area on Rorschach Card VI is seen as "Two laser guns—the tip of the gun, barrel, trigger, and handle." Rorschach IX—"Ink splattered all over a person's face."

V-12 Rage at insults: Steven told this author that he felt furious and set more fires after some of his peers taunted him and called him "Arsonist—burn your fingers off!" This relentless teasing and ostracism by the community began in June 1991, after his stepfather and he were arrested and exposed when the case made the local newspapers. Steven was hospitalized in March 1992, one day after his twelfth fire, set close to home. According to his mother, "The kids in school had been teasing Steven throughout the school year about setting fires. He got upset and angry by this. The community is scared of him."

V-13 Destruction of property. Steven set a total of 12 fires, most of which destroyed valuable property.

V-15 A five-year history of lighting numerous fires, both with his stepfather and alone.

V-16 He set fires intentionally and deliberately to communicate a message to his mother.

V-17 Among other motivations, such as anger at his parents for neglect and abandonment and rage at insults from peers, Steven's firesetting should also be understood as a cry for help and an act of misguided, illogical self-assertion to send a distress signal to his mother that he was being sexually abused.

V-20 Steven has poor peer relations. He is a loner, isolated, and often feels inadequate and scapegoated.

V-30 He has had limited parental supervision by the mother.

To gain a deeper theoretical understanding of Steven's vengeful attitude toward his stepfather, we draw on a discussion of boys who became severe firesetters after being sexually abused by men: "Boys who have been sexually violated harbor an enormous amount of rage. Their fantasies of violent rage are even more severe if the boys have been anally penetrated rather than orally copulated. Firesetting becomes, for these boys, the means of total eradication of the offending object. Criminal offenders who have been sexually exploited almost always link their firesetting with their sexual abuse." [Wooden and Berkey 1984:101-102]

In this connection, an earlier investigator [Kaufman 1962] wrote that to understand seriously disturbed and acting-out children who have set serious fires, "the ego mechanisms of externalization and identification with the aggressor are important. These ego mechanisms involve the transformation of the fear of being in the passive position and being overwhelmed by massive anxiety into the active process of destroying."

According to both his psychological profile and the prediction equation score of +1.04, Steven is at definite risk for future firesetting. He shares positive scores on the foregoing 14 variables with a group of 50 severe or pathological firesetters.

Steven, however, also shows certain characteristics (see below) that were found in our two control groups of 105 nonfiresetters and minor firesetters. The presence of these factors would tend to diminish his chances of setting more fires. We consider them to be ego strengths and control factors that would tend to inhibit acting out, including firesetting. First of all, conditions had changed. His secret was out, the abuser was in jail, and his mother finally got the message of his cry for help.

> V-5 It is diagnostically favorable that Steven's superego development was not truly deficient, and was being strengthened by his therapy in the hospital. That firesetting had become ego-alien for him was suggested by his answer to the sentence completion item: It burns me up that…"I started fires."

> V-7 He stated that he did not become sexually excited by the fires he lit, and he and his stepfather never had sex at the site of a fire.

> V-14 In answer to questions, he told me that he never felt inherently attracted to or fascinated by fires. There were also no fire or explosion responses projected on the Rorschach, and no fire symbolism was revealed in his drawings or sentence completion test. He did not dream or daydream about fires.

V-19 He expressed feelings of guilt or shame about his firesetting. The examining psychologist wrote in his report, "He appears appropriately remorseful for his actions." When he arrived at the hospital, he was depressed and expressed negative feelings about himself. In the interview, he told me that "firesetting is wrong because people could have been killed, and I, too, could have been trapped in the fire." It is noteworthy that he and his stepfather took care never to set fire to a building that was inhabited by people.

V-22 He has the ability to trust and relate to interested and accepting adults. He could form attachments, tended to hang around the adults on the ward, and looked for acceptance and approval from them.

V-24 As might be expected, he suffers from castration anxiety, or fear of bodily harm. He feels intimidated by authority figures and by "the Law."

V-25 He has shown no behavioral problems in school leading to suspension or expulsion. In fact, he is described as a good, though somewhat limited, student.

V-26 He has never been known to be cruel to animals or to other children.

V-27 Steven is capable of some empathy with others. He told the ward staff that he did not wish to harm anybody with his fires. That's why he chose only empty houses (see V-19).

V-28 He was not exposed to fire nor did he play with matches before the age of nine, when he was initiated into firesetting by the stepfather.

V-29 He is not enuretic.

Taking into account all the available evidence, it was possible to make an assessment and to come to a conclusion about Steven. His clinical record, his test results, and the interview material do closely resemble the psychological profile of the seriously at-risk firesetter. Initially, the fires were set reluctantly, because he was being coerced, bribed, and manipulated by his stepfather. He was very angry with his biological father, his mother, and his stepfather. No one was there to protect him. Later, beginning about age 13, he set some fires alone to attract attention to himself, or as a desperate, nonverbal communication to his mother. On the record, therefore, Steven's firesetting was a complex and overdetermined act that had a variety of dynamic meanings.

Finally, however, the consultant has to make sense of and integrate all these sometimes conflicting or contradictory data. Here, there is no substitute for sound, critical, clinical thinking that is supported by theory and by solid, up-to-date, research-derived data. In this perspective, Steven is quite *capable* of setting more fires were he to be discharged back into the community, but he is *unlikely* to do so.

To provide Steven with the necessary help and support, and to reduce the likelihood of further firesetting, the following steps were recommended to the hospital's treatment team for after Steven's discharge from the hospital:

1. He should continue to receive intensive individual outpatient therapy dealing with the abuse, with his psychological pain, and with the meaning of his firesetting.

2. He and his mother should have joint therapy appointments to improve the past poor communication between them.

3. Steven's mother should receive concurrent help to improve her parenting skills and to become more sensitive, open, and available to her son.

4. Finally, for at least a year, Steven should have to report regularly to his probation officer, to emphasize accountability and responsibility on his part, and to make clear to him that society takes a very dim view of arson. This will also remind him that "the Law" continues to look over his shoulder.

One could hope that with internal changes promoted by psychotherapy, and external structure and support provided by the community, Steven's prognosis for not returning to his past pattern of firesetting could be greatly improved.

Epilogue

Nine months after this evaluation, a follow-up phone call to Steven's social worker at the psychiatric hospital brought out the following: After the evaluation, Steven remained at the hospital for two more months and received both individual and group therapy. He was then placed in a residential school not far from his home. Meanwhile, his mother married for the third time and became quite involved with her new husband. She continued to be distant and ambivalent toward Steven. Sometimes she was "scared of him"; at other times she visited him or let him visit at home.

At the residential school, he kept to himself and was described as a loner. He continued to be teased by peers. After three months at the school, he set a fire in the community. The sequence was that he was teased and pushed around by some boys in his residence. He had off-grounds privileges, so he went for a walk "to cool off." A man shouted something at him from his porch (reason unknown). Later in the day, Steven returned with matches and set a fire on the man's porch that scorched the house. Five days later, he also set a fire in the bathroom of his school, at which time the school asked for his return to the hospital.

Although he received some therapy at the school, according to his social worker, he never discussed the sexual abuse he had suffered. Back in the hospital for the past four months, he is now talking about it to his therapist. With her help, he has also written a poignant letter to his abuser, who is still in prison, complaining about the way the man treated him. Because of his history of numerous fires, the hospital staff is now trying to place him in a residential treatment facility.*

The prediction equation and the psychological profile had classified Steven correctly as a boy who was a definite risk for further firesetting in the community. In our opinion, he regressed because he did not receive the intensive individual and family therapy that we and the psychiatric hospital's treatment team had recommended. Lonely, isolated, and vulnerable, he became enraged once more at insults, teasing, and disrespect from both peers and adults, and reverted back to expressing his accumulated anger and feelings of revenge by setting fires. He may also have signaled to his caregivers that he was unable to handle an open setting and required the tight structure and support that only a residential treatment facility can provide.

---

* In New York State, a residential treatment facility (RTF) is under the jurisdiction of the state Department of Mental Health, while a residential treatment center (RTC) is under the jurisdiction of the Department of Social Services. The former is a more highly structured, more secure, and more closely supervised facility for the treatment of seriously disturbed and acting-out children and adolescents. It has a higher staff-to-patient ratio than the RTC, tends to be smaller in size, and falls somewhere between an RTC and the closed children's ward of a psychiatric hospital.

Appendix:
Examples of Nonsevere and Severe Firesetters

NONSEVERE

1. While playing with matches, a seven-year-old boy set fire to some paper bags and cardboard boxes in the parking lot behind his house. His mother saw it and quickly extinguished it. (Playing with matches)

2. A five-year-old boy was left alone and unsupervised in a motel room while his mother went shopping. He felt bored, restless, and angry about being left alone. He played with matches and soon set the motel room on fire, burning it out and making himself, his mother, and his siblings homeless. (Playing with matches, call for help, anger at being left alone)

3. A 14-year-old boy, whose mother found him beyond her control and was trying to get him placed outside the home, lit numerous matches, let them burn out, and left them lying around the floor for his mother to find. He never set an actual fire or burned any object. He seemed to want to attract her attention by scaring the living daylights out of her. (He was angry about being placed, was protesting in his own way, but at the same time showed that he needed placement.)

4. After asking his social worker several times to remove him from a foster home where he was unhappy, a nine-year-old boy deliberately set a small fire in the foster home. He wanted to be placed in another foster home with an older sister who was living there. The foster mother asked the agency for his immediate removal. (Power struggle, manipulation, cry for help)

5. A mother reported that her seven-year-old son, with no previous history of firesetting, began to light matches and candles and to cut up family photographs right after his parents' divorce. He also lit a napkin on the stove. (Cry for help)

6. At the residential treatment center, a 14-year-old boy with no previous history of firesetting burned a newspaper and singed the door to the cottage

office. Later the same day, the cottage parent found him sitting outside the cottage next to a small fire burning on the road. He was looking at the fire and crying. The child care worker put out the fire and learned from the boy that he had just burned his mother's picture. He said he was angry with his mother for placing him. He felt abandoned by her. (Cry for help and anger at mother; he felt rejected and abandoned, and hurt and angry.)

7. At the residential treatment center, a 12-year-old boy of dull-normal intelligence set fire to his mattress to get attention. When interviewed about the incident by the unit administrator, he said, "I wanted to go home, and I thought if I had no bed you would send me home." (Seeking attention, manipulation, misinterpreting cause and effect)

8. A 16-year-old girl who was very attractive was being sexually harassed by her stepfather, who tried repeatedly to seduce her. She had a strong enough ego and superego to resist his advances. When she finally told her mother, her mother refused to believe her and accused her of trying to wreck her marriage "because you never liked him, were jealous, and didn't want me to marry him." Shortly thereafter, the girl set fire to a storage room adjacent to her stepfather's office in the building where he was superintendent. When she told her story to the police and to the representatives of the Department of Social Services, she was promptly removed from her home and placed at the residential treatment center. (Cry for help, anger at attempted sexual abuse and at her mother for failing to protect her)

SEVERE

1. After being reprimanded and put on cottage restriction, a 15-year-old schizophrenic boy deliberately set a neighboring school gymnasium on fire with paint thinner found on the building site, which he splashed all around, causing $500,000 worth of property damage. (Power struggle with authority, spite, and revenge)

2. During an ongoing feud with a cottagemate, a 16-year-old boy intentionally set fire with a lit cigarette to the other boy's locker while the group was at lunch. In half an hour, the entire upper floor of the cottage burned out and the children and staff members lost all their belongings. (Revenge and retaliation)

3. In a residential treatment center, a 16-year-old boy who had recently arrived from a psychiatric hospital set fire to his cottage. The cottage was destroyed, one boy was killed, and a girl was severely injured. (Revenge and displaced aggression against the RTC)

4. A boy who was four and a half years old set his house on fire. According to police reports, his mother had left him alone and unsupervised in her bedroom while she was in the bathroom abusing cocaine. He found her lighter, played with it, and set fire to her bed. Then he stood there and watched it for a while. When the flames became too big and too hot, he ran out and called for his mother. She grabbed him and was able to save him and herself. Her boyfriend, who lived downstairs, is a drug dealer. The child told the admitting physician in the emergency room that he wanted to burn the house down "because I hate the landlord." (Cry for help, wish to get his mother's care and attention, and undoubtedly anger at his mother's neglect and unavailability)

5. A 15-year-old boy set fire to an empty building belonging to a religious sect or cult that his parents had joined. His father regularly beat and abused him to make him conform and fall in line with the dictates of the tyrannical cult leader. When the boy was finally asked to leave the cult because of his "rebelliousness" and nonconformity, the father took him to live with the boy's aunt, who was the father's sister. The aunt was afraid to leave him at home alone because whenever he did not want to accept her house rules or curfew he threatened to set fire to her house. (Cry for help, power struggle with the aunt, and strong feelings of wanting to take revenge for months of severe physical abuse by his father)

6. A six-year-old boy deliberately set three fires at his mother's house and at his aunt's house. The staff of the psychiatric hospital where the boy was placed suspected physical or sexual abuse. The child heard voices telling him "to light things up." (Severely disturbed, psychotic firesetter with command hallucinations)

7. An eight-year-old boy was placed in a diagnostic center because he was beyond the control of the grandparents who were his caregivers. According to the case record, when he was an infant, his mother had "knowingly abandoned him and his siblings to her parents' care and the children think of their grandparents as their parents." He was placed in the diagnostic center because he was lying, stealing, running away from home, and had a history of match-play. In school, he got into trouble for fighting and for "stripping a little girl on her way home." Prior to placement, a very serious incident occurred when he set his grandfather's bed on fire while the grandfather was lying in it. The bewildered man told the psychiatrist, "He almost burned me up." The grandfather felt especially hurt since "we took him in as a baby and provided the only stable home he and his brothers and sisters have ever known." The grandparents were inconsistent in their treatment of him. The grandmother was kind, indulgent, and forgiving; the grandfather was described by the psychiatrist as "caring and involved, but also a disciplinarian, stands by his word, and believes in the use of punishment." The boy played one against the other.

This boy gave a remarkably original set of associations to Card III of the Rorschach. On this card, where human beings are usually seen in some sort of interaction, he projected the following response: "This looks like two people holding a pot over a fire. You see, two people picked up a pot. The red is the fire. A house got on fire. Somebody put a match; maybe he was mad at the person for throwing a brick through the window." When asked by the psychologist to clarify this response, he added, "The little kid was mad at the lady because she yelled at him. He broke her window, and threw a match inside the window and the house got on fire." (What happened then?) "He got in trouble. I'd do that. My face gets hot and red when I'm mad." The boy started out well enough with his initial perception, but soon his associations became more and more personalized and self-revealing. This was an unusually strong original fire association on the part of a severe firesetter. (We scored it for V-4, Revenge fantasy; V-8, Impulsivity or loss of control; V-11, Aggressive-destructive fantasy; V-14, Fire attraction or preoccupation with acting out of hostility; and V-27, lack of empathy with others.)

The same boy also saw Card IX as a fire. "I said a fire, right! The fire is blowing up. It really looks like the devil with pointy things sticking out." (Scored for V-14, Fire attraction, and V-8, Impulsivity)

References

American Psychiatric Association (APA). *Diagnostic and Statistical Manual of Mental Disorders,* 3rd Edition (DSM III). Washington, DC: APA, 1980.

Awad, George, and Harrison, J. "Single Case Study. A Female Firesetter: A Case Report." *Journal of Nervous and Mental Disease* 163, 6 (1976): 432–437.

Block, J.H., and Block J. "Fire and Young Children: Learning Survival Skills." Berkeley, CA: Technical Report for the Pacific Southwest Forest Range, 1975.

Bumpass, Eugene R.; Fagelman, F.D.; and Brix, R.J. "Intervention with Children Who Set Fires." *American Journal of Psychotherapy* 37 (1983): 328-345.

Chess, Stella, and Hassibi, M. *Principles and Practice of Child Psychiatry.* New York: Plenum Press, 1978, 128-129.

Cole, R.E.; Grolnick, W.S.; and Laurentis, L.R. *Children and Fire: Rochester Fire-Related Youth Progress Report.* Rochester, NY: Rochester Fire Department, 1986.

Eisler, Richard M. "Crisis Intervention in the Family of a Firesetter." *Psychotherapy: Theory, Research and Practice* 9, 1 (Spring 1972): 76–79.

Fine, Stuart, and Louie, Don. "Juvenile Firesetters: Do the Agencies Help?" *American Journal of Psychiatry* 136, 4A (1979): 433-435.

Fineman, Kenneth R. "Firesetting in Childhood and Adolescence." *Psychiatric Clinics of North America* 3, 3 (1980): 483-500.

Gaynor, Jessica, and Hatcher, Carl. *The Psychology of Child Firesetting.* New York: Bruner/Mazel, 1987.

Grolnick, Wendy; Cole, Robert; Laurentis, Lauretta; and Schwartzman, P. "Playing with Fire: A Developmental Assessment of Children's Fire Understanding and Experience." *Journal of Clinical Child Psychology* 19, 2 (1990): 128-135.

Gruber, Allen R.; Heck, Edward T.; and Mintzer, Ellen. "Children Who Set Fires: Some Background and Behavioral Characteristics." *American Journal of Orthopsychiatry* 51, 3 (1981): 484-488.

Heath, G. Adair; Hardesty, Vaughn A.; Goldfine, Peter E.; and Walker, Alexander M. "Childhood Firesetting: An Empirical Study." *Journal of the American Academy of Child Psychiatry* 22, 4 (1983): 370-374.

Jacobson, Robin, R. "The Subclassification of Child Firesetters." *Journal of Child Psychology and Psychiatry* 26, 5 (1985): 759-767.

Juvenile Firesetter Intervention Program (JFIP). *1988: First Annual Report.* New York: New York City Fire Department, 1989.

Kafrey, D. "Playing with Matches, Children and Fire." *Fires and Human Behavior,* edited by D. Canter. New York: John Wiley and Sons, 1980.

Kaufman, Irving. "Crimes of Violence and Delinquency in Schizophrenic Children." *Journal of the American Academy of Child Psychiatry* 1, 2 (1962): 269-283.

Kaufman, I.; Heims, L.W.; and Reiser, D.E. "A Re-evaluation of the Psychodynamics of Firesetting." *American Journal of Orthopsychiatry* 31 (1961): 123-136.

Kerlinger, F.N. *Foundations of Behavior Research.* New York: Holt, Rinehart, and Winston, 1973.

Kolko, David J. "Juvenile Firesetting: A Review and Methodological Critique." *Clinical Psychology Review* 31, 5 (1985): 345-376.

Kolko, David J. "Firesetting and Pyromania." Chapter 22 in *Handbook of Child Psychiatric Diagnosis,* edited by C.G. Last and M. Hensen. New York: John Wiley and Sons, 1989.

Kolko, David J., and Kazdin, A. "The Emergence and Recurrence of Child Firesetting: A One-Year Prospective Study." *Journal of Abnormal Child Psychology* 20, 1 (1992): 17–37.

Koson, D.F., and Dvoskin, J. "Arson: A Diagnostic Study." *Bulletin of the American Academy of Psychiatry and Law* 10 (1982): 39-49.

Lewis, N., and Yarnell, H. "Pathological Firesetting." *Nervous and Mental Disease Monographs* 82 (1951).

Lowenstein, L.F. "The Diagnosis of Child Arsonists." *Acta Paedopsychiatrica* 47, 3 (1981): 151-154.

Macht, Lee B., and Mack, John E. "The Firesetter Syndrome." *Psychiatry* 31 (1968): 287.

Murray, H.A. *Thematic Apperception Test*. Cambridge: Harvard University Press, 1943.

Nichtern, Sol, M.D. Personal communication, 1984.

Nurcombe, B. "Children Who Set Fires." *Medical Journal of Australia* 1 (1964): 579-584.

Rorschach, Herman. *Psychodiagnostics*. Berne, Switzerland: Verlag Hans Huber, 1942.

Sakheim, George A.; Vigdor, M.G.; Gordon, M.; and Helprin, L. "A Psychological Profile of Juvenile Firesetters in Residential Treatment." *CHILD WELFARE* LXIV, 5 (1985): 453-476.

Sakheim, George A., and Osborn, Elizabeth: "A Psychological Profile of Juvenile Firesetters in Residential Treatment: A Replication Study." *CHILD WELFARE* LXV, 5 (1986): 495-503.

Sakheim, George A.; Osborn, Elizabeth; and Abrams, D. "Toward a Clearer Differentiation of High-Risk from Low-Risk Firesetters." *CHILD WELFARE* LXX, 4 (1991): 489–503.

Siegelman, E.Y., and Folkman, W.S. "Youthful Firesetters: An Exploratory Study in Personality and Background." Springfield VA: U.S.D.A. Forest Service, 1971.

Stewart, Mark A., and Culver, Kenneth W. "Children Who Set Fires: The Clinical Picture and a Follow-Up." *British Journal of Psychiatry* 140 (1982): 357-363.

U.S. Federal Bureau of Investigation. *Crime in the United States*. Washington, DC: U.S. Government Printing Office, 1987.

Vandersall, Thornton A., and Welner, Jerry M. "Children Who Set Fires." *Archives of General Psychiatry* 22 (January 1970): 63-71.

Vreeland, Robert G., and Levin, Bernard M. "Psychological Aspects of Firesetting." In *Fires and Human Behavior,* ed. by D. Canter. New York: John Wiley and Sons, Ltd., 1980.

Webb, Nancy B.; Sakheim, G.A.; Towns-Miranda, L.; and Wagner, Charles R. "Collaborative Treatment of Juvenile Firesetters: Assessment and Outreach." *American Journal of Orthopsychiatry* 60, 2 (April 1990): 305–310.

Wechsler, David. *Wechsler Intelligence Scale for Children—Revised*. New York: Harcourt, Brace and Jovanovich, Inc., 1974.

Welsh, R.S. "The Use of Stimulus Satiation in the Elimination of Juvenile Firesetting Behavior." In *Behavior Therapy with Children,* edited by A. Graziani. Chicago, IL: Aldine Atherton Press, 1971.

Wooden, Wayne S., and Berkey, Martha L. *Children and Arson: America's Middle Class Nightmare.* New York: Plenum, 1984.

Yarnell, Helen: "Firesetting in Children." *American Journal of Orthopsychiatry* 10 (1940): 272-286.

Yates, F. *Statistics for the Social Sciences,* 2nd edition. New York: Holt, Rinehart, and Winston, Inc., 1973.

About the Authors

George A. Sakheim, Ph.D., is a clinical psychologist in private practice who specializes in the assessment of juvenile and adolescent firesetters. He has published and presented widely in this specialty, and serves as a consultant to the Westchester County Department of Social Services, the county's Family Court, the Westchester County Medical Center, the New York State Office of Developmental Disabilities and Mental Retardation, and a number of residential treatment centers in the greater New York area. His long career as psychologist and clinical director in residential facilities included 16 years as chief psychologist at the Pleasantville Cottage School, Jewish Child Care Association of New York. In 1945–'46, he served as an interpreter at the Nuremberg war crimes trials.

Elizabeth Osborn, Ph.D., is a clinical psychologist in private practice with adults and children in Westchester County, New York, and Fairfield County, Connecticut. She is also director of the Child Guidance Center and coordinator of psychological services for the Pleasantville campus, Jewish Child Care Association of New York. Osborn received her doctorate from Fordham University, and has worked in the field of child welfare for 10 years. In addition to work on the subject of juvenile firesetting, she has published research on the treatment of opiate addiction.